# UNDERNEATH NEW YORK

*Also by* HARRY GRANICK

RUN! RUN!
*A mystery adventure through*
*New York's streets*

# Underneath
# New York

by

Harry Granick

Diagrams by

Philip Westerfield May

New York • RINEHART & COMPANY, INC. • Toronto

*To the two thousand years of scientists, engineers and workers whose labor made possible the modern city, and to the scientists, engineers, workers and good citizens of today and tomorrow who will make the cities of the future centers of health, ease of living, beauty and peaceful activity.*

# CONTENTS

## LIST OF ILLUSTRATIONS

# PART I

## WHAT IS IT ALL ABOUT?

## Chapter 1

## What Is It All About?

FEW PLACES ARE MORE FASCINATING than a hole in the ground. But a hole in a city street—that is in a class by itself!

Gaze down it. Look at the maze of timbers and steel beams; the huge pipes, the narrow tubes, the cables, the tunnels that dive into mysterious dark. Look at the men digging, drilling, sawing, riveting, pouring concrete; the monstrous power machines that grind, mix, load, unload, carry. A din of vast dangerous labors hangs over the excavation.

What is going on down there? Is it important?

For answer, shoot up with me to the observation gallery of the Empire State, the tallest building in New York City.

Below us, flung out among the busy waters of three rivers, a bay and a sound, is the most gigantic single community in the history of man. Eight million people live in it, more people than in fifteen states of our Union put together. We look down upon the hundreds of thousands of residences, stores, factories, office and government buildings which house them. Our eyes run along the grid of streets and elevated railroads. We gaze out upon green parks and beaches sparkling in the distance. We note monuments, museums and spires.

There is the City, we think, a grand stirring spectacle! There it is spread out below us, every bit of it!

Every bit of it?

Of course not!

For even as your brain, nerves, heart, lungs and stomach are hidden from view, so it is with the City. Its nervous system, the vital organs which provide it with heat, water, light and air, its intestines, which like yours, eliminate its wastes, its great arteries of rapid transit, which like yours, carry its stream of life to all ends of its body, all these and more that make it possible for eight million people to live together, are out of sight under the pavements and the waterways.

But why is this complicated machine buried under tons of concrete and water where it is so hard to get at? Well, do you wear your heart upon your sleeve? No. It beats under the protection of a cage of ribs and muscle. The mechanism of the City also is too delicate and too vital to be placed out in the open. Not only would it be in constant danger, but it would also menace the lives of the people about it. Gas, electricity, water and steam are useful only under control. Accidents do happen. Once on the loose, these forces can kill.

There are other good reasons for their being where they are. City streets would have to be six or eight times their present width to accommodate the vast network. Pipes and cables would have to skip up into the air above all crossings. Streets would look cluttered and messy. They would have less light. No. Decidedly, and from all points of view the machinery of the City had better stay where it is. It is safer underground. Our comfort, yes, our very lives depend on its ability to function twenty-four hours a day every day.

Perhaps, when you were very young, you did not bother your head about sources. You assumed that water came out of the faucet; that slops vanished down the drain; that electricity came from the button on the wall; that the gas was stored in the meter; that the spirit of the telephone was somehow imprisoned in the box to which the instrument is attached; that the telegram for your father was merely a message brought by the messenger boy.

But suppose one morning, you woke up and found that a giant power had snatched the entire underground from under you!

Your radio would not tell you that because there would be no electricity to operate it. Your father would fume because for the same reason, the newspaper presses had not been able to get out the morning paper to tell him what happened here or anywhere in the world.

You go to the bathroom, the faucets are dry. There is no water to flush the bowl. Your mother, trying hard to get breakfast for you and father, is baffled. She can't cook the cereal, she can't heat coffee or milk, the toaster remains cold. There is your shirt to iron, but the iron is useless.

Angered, your father calls upon the superintendent. The super does not know what's wrong. The whole block is in the same fix, he reports. "We'll see about that!" storms your father. "It's outrageous! I'll telephone the Health Department." He picks up the receiver; he dials operator. There is no answer. The wire is dead.

Unwashed, breakfastless, you join the people milling about on the street. Nobody knows what has happened.

"Well," says father, "I can't stay here all day. I'll be late to work." He goes off to the subway. In a few minutes, he is back. No trains are running. The "El" is at a standstill. So are the street cars. Few buses are about; the supply of gasoline and oil is being reserved for emergency use by the Police and Fire Departments and ambulances.

You trot off to school. There are no teachers and therefore no classes. That is perhaps the only bright spot in your life at the moment until you remember that you are hungry, thirsty and dirty, and that everyone about you is frightened.

At lunch and in the evening you get cold food out of cans. There is no bread because there is no water.

Your mother has expected a letter. It does not arrive. The Post Office, like your school, is understaffed; its underground mail chutes have vanished. In desperation, your father decides to send a telegram asking your out-of-town uncle whether the family can visit him during the trouble. The telegraph office is closed. There are no wires along which to send telegrams.

You go to sleep early because your mother has been able to buy only one candle for light. Most stores have never sold candles.

The next morning is even worse. There is a look of terror on everyone's face. The streets are foul with garbage and human wastes. Food is becoming scarce. Food in your home, in stores, in warehouses is rotting for lack of refrigeration. Your father's newspaper, now reduced to handbill size and printed on a hand press, reports factories closed; hospital service almost at an end for lack of water, light and proper sanitation. Fires are raging in many parts of the city. There is looting and violence because the police cannot be promptly notified and because all burglary alarms are useless. And worst of all and most terrifying, typhoid fever is breaking out due to drinking the dirty river water.

In a week or less, what with thirst, hunger, filth and disease— well, perhaps this is a good place to stop. No such tragedy is likely. The underground mechanism is well protected. But you can see that life in the city would be absolutely impossible without it.

That is why people are more likely to stare down the holes in New York City streets than to crane their necks up at the magnificent towers that rise above them.

Many of them would like to know more about the tremendous organism. They would like to know who were its inventors, how it was developed, how it was built, what it does, who pays for it. They would like to know more about the men who work underground and under water, the sandhogs and the divers. They would like to know what cities were like before the burst of inventions made the modern city possible. Unfortunately, the engineers who know the answers have thus far been too busy to tell us. When they write, they write only for engineers. The underground machine is mainly their secret.

Well, I like a secret, but only when I know it. I suppose you feel the same way. That is why, with great quantities of generous help, I am writing this book. You and I are going to explore underneath New York City together.

But before we begin—are you a member of the S.S.C.?

I will tell you a story.

One day, Mr. John D. Rockefeller, Jr., whose money helped build the famous group of New York City buildings known as Radio City, put his eye to a knothole in a fence separating the sidewalk from the deep foundation of his newest skyscraper. Every knothole in the fence had a curious eye screwed into it. Suddenly a workman waving a red flag came down the walk.

"Move on!" he cried. "We're going to blast!"

Mr. Rockefeller did not budge. After all it was his skyscraper.

"Move on," shouted the man at him. "You want to get hurt?"

"Say," warned a shabby bystander, "that's Mr. Rockefeller you're talking to."

"Oh yeah?" snapped the workman. "And I suppose you're

Mr. Morgan? Beat it, the two of you! We're blasting."

Mr. Rockefeller moved on. But he was indignant. Why couldn't he be allowed to watch the work? It was not only the drilling and blasting. Later on would come the job of feeding all the underground services into the new building. He knew there were thousands of people a day whose curiosity was being shut off as his had been. He talked to the builder.

As a result, the wooden fence was replaced by a heavy wire mesh through which many more people could survey the scene without danger. The new gallery was called the Sidewalk Superintendents' Club. Every one who stopped to stare down at the foundation was invited to sign a card and become a member of the S.S.C.

That was in 1938.

But the institution of Sidewalk Superintendents is one of the oldest in the world. Undoubtedly, King Solomon was one of its earliest members. Perhaps you too belong to it. Indeed, after you have read this book, you may begin signing your name with a comma and the initials M.S.S.C. after it, meaning: Member, Sidewalk Superintendents' Club.

## Chapter 2

### Not So Long Ago

*Lost, the art of bathing, somewhere in the Roman Empire. Has not been seen for fourteen hundred years. Finder please return to the* GREAT UNWASHED WORLD.

YOU MAY NOT UNDERSTAND this advertisement. But had your father's grandfather seen it, he would have known it to be true.

H. L. Mencken once wrote a story about an Adam Thompson of Cincinnati, Ohio, who presumably was one of the first to discover the missing article. He had built a bathtub in his home, a nice generous tub as big as a double bed and weighing as much as a prize bull.

On a cold December day in 1842, he invited a few friends to celebrate the occasion by taking the first tubbing in America.

Next day the newspapers were full of descriptions of what
they considered a shameful event.  They wrote that Mr. Thompson
thought more of his body than of his soul, that he had set a horrible
example of indecency, and they hoped he would be punished by
catching his death of cold.  The whole town was upset.

Years later, Mencken laughed at his readers for believing this
story.  But, though he had invented the incident, the physical and
moral distaste for bathing was true to the time.  Virginia tried to
discourage bathing by a tax of thirty dollars on every bathtub
brought into the state.  Boston, then the hub of American culture,
demanded a doctor's prescription before it would permit a person
to bathe.

I tell you this in order to remind you that the world has not
always been as you see it today.

Man has been a creature of the earth a long time; some say
a hundred thousand years.  Some say more than a million years.
But many of the things we know today, we learned only in the last
hundred years.

Talk to your parents.  They will tell you that the automobile,
the airplane, the moving picture, the radio came in their time.
The chances are good that they can remember gas lighting in their
homes and iron stoves for heating and cooking.  Perhaps they can
even remember streetcars drawn by horses.

They will tell you that most homes had no bathrooms.  Many
tenement house toilets were in the yards from which foul odors
sifted into homes and streets.  The phrase, "cleanliness is next to
godliness," was just beginning to take hold.

For centuries the peoples of the earth were swept by vast waves
of plagues that often traveled five and ten thousand miles before
their force was spent.  Millions upon millions died.  At times, a
third of the population of the known world would be destroyed by
one long, merciless wave.

No one knew the cause of disease.  Some people thought
demons were to blame.  Others thought it was the Evil Eye.  Still
others believed that plagues were due to the just wrath of God.
Many of the wise men said that disease was brought by great winds,

or by stinking fogs, or by cloud bursts, or by long droughts, or by the conjunction of the stars.

But neither devil-charms, nor magic, nor the torture of witches, neither prayers nor sacrifices could break the onslaught of the plagues. Not until the germ was discovered were the peoples of the earth able to protect themselves intelligently.

Louis Pasteur was the man who first proved the connection between germs and disease. But two hundred years before him, a little Dutch janitor, Anton Van Leeuwenhoek had made a microscope strong enough to see the germs. After Pasteur came many keen men who found out more and more about germs and how to fight them. Paul de Kruif, in an inspiring book called *Microbe Hunters,* tells about these brave scientists, some of whom were slain while pursuing the invisible enemies of mankind.

These scientists may have disagreed on many points, but they were united on one observation: *Dirt and impure water breed most of the pestilences that afflict man.* And from that they concluded that water, just plain clean water to drink, to bathe in, and to wash cities clean, is man's greatest protector of health and guarantor of life.

Astonishing, isn't it, that the world should have had to wait so long before finding out something that is now plain to the youngest among us!

But since that is so, what were cities like long ago?

If you will look back at the advertisement which heads this chapter, you will notice that cleanliness was practiced by the civilized world fifteen hundred years ago.

Sir Arthur Keith, archeologist, reports on Mohenjo-daro, buried by time under the bank of the Indus River and now being dug into the light of day. "As regards sanitary engineering, this city of ancient Sind led the way. No city that can claim five thousand years, so nearly approached our modern standard of sanitation as does Mohenjo-daro." He thereupon describes the well-laid bathrooms with toilets in the corners. Vertical pipes carried the wastes down the brick drains which connected with the capacious main sewers, evenly graded downward under arched brick roofs.

The great civilization of ancient Egypt knew the value of cleanliness and pure water. Near the Pyramid of Gizeh is a well dug through solid rock to a depth of three hundred feet. Many Egyptian cities brought water from afar in solidly built aqueducts or waterways. They built sewers. Their people believed in bathing. They honored the men who taught them how to live in good health. Imhotep, the first physician in known history, had a temple erected in his honor. He was worshipped as a god, five thousand years ago.

The ancient Hebrews, following the laws of Moses, have been called the real founders of the science of Public Health. The Bible relates that Moses was "learned in all the wisdom of the Egyptians." They not only stressed the importance of cleanliness but they tried to control the spread of disease by keeping the healthy away from the sick. Sometimes, the house of the sick was torn down and its materials borne out of the gates of the city.

In 1918, an amazing palace on the Island of Crete was dug out of the oblivion of four thousand years. It had bathrooms and toilets all properly connected to a central sewer.

But it was Rome, conqueror of the ancient world, which brought the whole idea of pure water, personal cleanliness and clean cities to the highest point of perfection. The Romans built magnificent public baths, with hot and cold water, large enough to hold three thousand people. Most Romans bathed at least once a day. By the time the northern barbarians overran Rome, the city was being fed by twenty tunnels of water, many of them carried by bridges across the valleys between hills. Some brought water from a mile away, some brought it ten miles, 43 miles, and one even brought it 61 miles. Each aqueduct drew its supply from a huge main reservoir and thence fed it into small local reservoirs in the city. Well-to-do Romans had their home wants supplied by lead pipes from the local reservoirs to their own cisterns, or sunken tanks. Poorer people drew their water from the hundreds of public fountains.

Four hundred years before Rome stopped drinking Tiber water and well water and the rain water collected in cisterns, it had built a splendid system of sewers. Most houses had a drain directly connected to the street sewer. However, since those drains did not reach above the first floor, people living in the upper stories often threw their slops out of the windows into the street. Not so nice;

but I have, myself, dodged garbage thrown from New York City apartment windows.

So well did the Romans build, that some of their aqueducts are still in use. The Cloaca Maxima, a sewer famous twenty-six hundred years ago, still helps to keep modern Rome clean.

In 452 A.D., the gates of this civilization gave way and the ferocious North European hordes swept into the city like a devouring flood. They destroyed everything they could not understand. They destroyed knowledge, art, literature, the science of healing and engineering. They destroyed the vital lesson humanity had learned of the importance of pure water and of personal and community hygiene. They drove time back to their own barbaric level.

Europe entered a period of about eight hundred years of ignorance, of superstition and of unspeakable filth. Our feeling about that long night in history is expressed by the name we have given it: The Dark Ages.

The ancient world, in spite of its knowledge and practice of elementary sanitation, had nevertheless been troubled by plagues. But its suffering and loss of life from disease was scarcely to be compared to the ravages of plague throughout the Dark Ages and the Middle Ages which followed.

When the Black Death struck Europe between 1343 and 1348, killing one third of its population, many people blamed it on an invisible giant riding an invisible black horse.

For almost five hundred years longer, Europe was revisited by the Black Death, by cholera, by the dread sweating diseases, and by other epidemics too numerous to recount. And still it made very little effort to clean up its cities. The simple rule of cleanliness lay buried under the rubble of antiquity.

In 1665, the teeming city of London still used its streams and the rivers Thames and Fleet as its main sewers. Three hundred years earlier, the Fleet had become so choked with filth and garbage that ships could no longer use it. The stench of these open sewers was overpowering. Had you lived then, you would have held your handkerchief to your nose, had a handkerchief been one of your prized possessions.

Nevertheless, people obtained their water largely from the sewery Thames and from the wells which could not store clean water out of springs fed by the wastes of a congested city. The two reservoirs, which had been built in 1609 and 1630, made very little difference to the city as a whole.

Most streets were unpaved. So far as possible, ladies and gentlemen went about on horseback or were carried in chairs to avoid stepping into mud or the filth of kitchen and toilet bucket hurled into the street. When Sir Walter Raleigh spread his cloak before good Queen Bess, it undoubtedly covered more than a mere puddle of water. Streets were lit on dark nights only. The law specified certain hours of such nights during which every house owner was obliged to hang out a horn lantern with a burning candle.

Homes, of course, were lighted by candles and heated by open hearths. Cooking was done over the hearth. Toilets were usually in the yard and there were no baths in an age which could face the terrors of the seven seas more calmly than the thought of washing one's body. Fresh air was considered a carrier of all ills. Therefore, windows were kept tightly locked against it.

It was this London that the Black Plague struck for the last time in 1665.

Johannes Nohl, in his book, "The Black Death," describes the terrifying picture for us, from the account of an eye-witness:

"When in London in July 1665 about two thousand died every week, most houses were closed, and the streets were empty. Only great fires were to be seen everywhere, which had been lighted for the purification of the air, and, with the exception of the men who with carts and coffins came to fetch the corpses, no living being was to be seen. On the house doors red crosses were painted with the inscription: 'Lord have mercy upon us.' Nothing was to be heard save the wailing of the dying, the lamenting of the relations, the tolling of the bell for those about to be buried, and the mournful call: 'Bring out your dead!'"

The following year, London suffered another historic blow. Fire destroyed four-fifths of the walled city. There was not enough water with which to fight the ravenous red devil nor sufficient force with which to shoot the water forth.

On the outskirts of the narrow, twisting, overcrowded alleys of Cairo, Egypt, is the Deserted City. Once I walked through its crumbled streets. There was no one, absolutely no one about.

Not even a dog. The white dwellings reflected the intense glare of the sun. No one had entered these houses for sixty years. I looked through the open gateways. I saw white graves and, painted upon them, the ancient signs of death by plague, crosses of blood. Suddenly, fear seemed to sit on every roof. I hastened away. Soon I was standing in an open field. I recognized the shallow pits into which garbage and human muck were once thrown for the hogs to consume.

Here, before my eyes, was the cause of the plague that had driven out those whom it had not destroyed. Filth. Lack of sewers. Undoubtedly, water made impure by the seepage of unclean matter through the thin, sandy soil.

This had happened when your grandfather was a young man. But Cairo was not the first city that had to flee the consequences of its disregard of simple sanitary rules. Many cities before it had to pick themselves up and find new sites. There are today many cities in Asia, and in Africa, whose people still have to learn what their ancestors knew thousands of years ago: *Pure water for drinking and water for cleaning is life.*

## Chapter 3

### Science And Invention To The Rescue

FIRST COMES THE DREAM. Then comes the method of making the dream come true. Possibly the oldest of all man's dreams is the dream of good health. There probably never was a time when man did not hope that all sickness would vanish from the earth.

Imhotep did something to make that hope come true. Moses strove mightily to teach man the rules of good living. Hippocrates, the Greek, called the father of the art of healing, put aside devils and gods, and tried to find out the natural reasons for man's illnesses. The engineers of the ancient world worked hard in the interests of health.

Even during the Dark Ages, when ignorance and superstition drew a blanket of filth and disease over the world, there were men who dreamed of a day when the world would awaken, throw off the brutal wrapping and arise keen and glowing. The dark dawn of that day was the Renaissance. The tremendous genius of two men gave it its first light. Leonardo da Vinci and Andreas Vesalius began once more the interrupted study of the body of man.

Wouldn't you suppose that these brilliant pioneers in the science of health were honored by the men of their time? The sad truth is that the wonderful anatomical drawings which Leonardo made were not published for four hundred years! When, in 1543, the great work of Vesalius appeared, such a roar went up against him for daring to challenge the existing body of knowledge that the bewildered young man burnt the rest of his notes and retired to a useless life. The graybeards of medicine did not wish to be told that they had a great deal to learn.

Nevertheless, the young physicians were paying less and less attention to the graybeards. They not only continued to examine the structure of the human body, but they began the study of how it works.

Then curious old Leeuwenhoek presented the world of science with its most important tool—the microscope. The world of the unseen was at once invaded and spied upon by hundreds of men hungry for the least scrap of fact. Germs were discovered. When Pasteur proved that certain kinds of germs cause disease, and showed how to combat those germs, man's dream of good health entered the stage of action.

And not a whit too soon. For over a hundred years before Pasteur, the world had been changing its manner of making things. Machines were being invented to take the place of handicrafts. Production in the home and in the tiny shop gave way to production in ever larger factories. The factories were in the cities. They needed ever more and more workers. Country men and women flocked into the cities. Families had more children, because more workers were needed. The cities grew enormously. They became more crowded, more dirty and more dangerous to health.

In 1800, London had a population of one million; by 1850, it had three million. In 1800, Manhattan Island had sixty thousand people; fifty years later it had almost nine times as many. The problems of health and sanitation became three, six, ten times as important—and as difficult.

It was England with its fearfully congested cities which made the first important move in the direction of public health. Already, after the London fire of 1666, men like Christopher Wren, the architect and city planner, noticed that disease seemed to attack the poor of the city first. In 1842, Edwin Chadwick of the Poor Law Commission published a most startling report. This report showed that one of the reasons for the poor being the greatest sufferers was the horrible filth in which they were forced to live and work.

So clearly did the report prove this, that everywhere cities began to survey their own conditions and to think of doing something about them.

New York City was one of the most overcrowded and filthy of all cities. Until 1842, its water came from brackish street wells. Its sewers were the streams. Huge piles of ashes, garbage and animal wastes fouled the streets. For over two hundred years, pigs, sometimes as many as twenty thousand, were the street cleaners. Charles Dickens did not like New York because of them. Fifth Avenue and Madison Avenue and Park Avenue, above 59th Street, depended on pigs until after the Civil War. During heavy rains, the disease-ridden slops from sick rooms and hospitals floated on the streets and were washed into homes. The city was visited by plagues every few years: in 1841, 1863, 1871, 1883, 1891, 1893. Tuberculosis, typhoid, diphtheria and dysentery killed thousands.

Something had to be done.

Soon after 1865, a Department of Health and a Bureau of Sanitation were set up. It was a beginning, but only a beginning. What the city needed first and above all was a larger supply of pure water and a sewer system. And it needed it quickly! By 1900, its population would grow to three and a malf million; by 1920, to five and a half million; by 1940, to eight million.

But New York City is not built on sand or a deep layer of earth. Its backbone is tough. You can see it sticking through its hide in a line that runs through Central Park, through Morningside Park, through the Terrace, east of New York City College, and on through the hills of Washington Heights. Curiously enough, it is spotted by one hundred and seventy varieties of precious and semi-precious stones, among them, garnets, amethysts, opals, beryls, tourmalines. In the American Museum of Natural History, you may see the largest garnet crystal ever found in the U.S.A. It came out of a ditch in West 35th Street, and for some time was used as a doorstep! Other minerals are also part of the basic rock. No. Manhattan schist, sparkling with mica and hardened by granite is not easily cut through.

But rock is not the only natural obstacle. Almost as difficult to overcome are underground springs and streams and sucking sand-whirls.

You remember what the ancients had been able to accomplish with the most primitive tools, the pick, the shovel, the lever and the wedge. On our own continent, the civilized Aztecs, whom the Spanish conquistadors destroyed cruelly, had bored a shaft one hundred feet down and from there, half a mile horizontally under the earth to a spring of pure water.

Why, then, could not New York City in the last half of the Nineteenth Century use its hand tools as well as the Aztecs and the Romans? It could. But it would have been an exceedingly long and costly job. The ancients used slave labor. They had no reason to hurry. The cities created by the Machine Age had every reason to hurry. They were doubling and tripling in size even while the City Fathers were arguing about methods, plans and costs.

However, the Machine Age, while creating problems, also came forward with the means to solve them. A triple play from scientist to inventor to engineer did the trick. The scientist did the research and supplied the theories. The inventor took these theories and turned them into machines which produced mechanical power to take the place of animal power, power tools to take the place of hand tools, and new materials as well as improvements on the old. With these, the engineer attacked the gigantic tasks of the New Age, and, in his own language, "licked the job"!

Don't think, however, that this marvelous team did its work overnight. True, the results of its labors are only 50 to 75 years old. But its work has a history that often goes back to the wonderful people of antiquity.

Since science is the knowledge of the facts of the universe, its materials and forces, the first tools of the scientist are his five senses and the theory of numbers. We owe the basis of the art of mathematics to the merchants and astrologers and architects of ancient Egypt, Phoenicia and Greece.

The fact is that history is like an assembly belt in an automobile factory. Some of its parts travel a long long time, before their significance becomes apparent in the machine of progress.

Our age has given us tremendous mechanical power. Yet the basis of the science of steam power, for which we are wont to give James Watt first credit, can be traced as far back as the Second Century, B.C., when Hero, a Greek mathematician, designed a toy steam pump for raising water. The steam turbine, as we know it, came into use in 1883.

Electric power was first used commercially in 1879. We at once think of Nikola Tesla, Thomas Edison and Charles Steinmetz. But their brilliant work was the end result of a long line of scientists that began with Thales of Miletus in 600 B.C.

The gasoline engine which not only drives our automobiles, but is used to provide power for tools, was invented by Dr. N. A. Otto in 1876. Dozens of men before him, however, provided the science and the principles which made his invention possible.

The use of the force of water, or hydraulic power, is the most ancient of all our power energies. The Egyptians used it to pump water into their irrigation ditches. The Greeks and Romans used it to force the water of their fountains to jet upward. The man with the most famous name in this science is Archimedes, who studied it in 250 B.C. It remained, however, for the Machine Age to harness its laws effectively.

Another force which our Age has learned to use is compressed air. In 1865, George Law of England patented the first tool employing compressed air. It was a rock drill, and a mighty important tool at a time when cities were thinking of building aqueducts and sewers. You will see later on in our story the tremendous importance of compressed air in the construction of underwater tunnels.

Not the least of the forces which aid modern construction is contained in dynamite. Its invention in 1862 repeats the great tragedy which so often faces the scientist and inventor. Alfred

Bernhard Nobel invented the explosive in order to help build a better world.  Just so, the Wright Brothers worked on the airplane to give men wings.  These men lived to see their inventions of good will converted by other men into instruments of death and destruction. Nobel was so shocked by the evil he had unloosed that he left a vast sum of money to be used in encouraging the arts of peace and the will to a peaceful world.  You may have heard of the Nobel prizes. Today, scientists and inventors are beginning to rebel at the harmful use to which their work is sometimes put.

This is not the book in which to do more than mention a few of the new materials invented by the chemists of our times and so vital to the construction of the underground services.  There is steel, which is a combination of iron and carbon; its many alloys, giving it lightness or flexibility or great heat resistance.  There is asbestos, rubber, Portland cement.

Using these materials and many more which the chemists have made, using the mechanized energy that the scientists and inventors have provided, employing the new power tools, drills, pumps, riveters, cranes, shovels, dynamite and compressed air, the construction engineers have gone to work with great imagination to make the ancient dream of healthy cities come true.

More than that, they have constructed for the expanding cities of the Machine Age the complex underground of transit and communications along which their life moves.

Let's have a look at their magnificent Machine for Living.

# PART II

# SANITATION

## Chapter 4

## Through The Faucet

BEFORE WATER COULD REACH your faucet, it had first to be found, then brought to a storage point and from there piped to your home. It seems as simple as walking.

But put yourself in the place of an engineer on the Board of Water Supply of the City of New York. It is the job of that Board to locate the water, to build the system which will convey it, and to turn this system over, complete and ready for use, to the Department of Water Supply, Gas and Electricity which will operate it.

One day, the Commissioners of your Board receive a letter.

Dear Sirs:

After very careful study, our engineers have come to the conclusion that the City has only enough sources of water supply to take care of its needs for the next twenty years.

23

By then, our population will have grown so large that we will require an additional five hundred million gallons a day. This extra amount will do us nicely until we write you a similar letter some twenty or twenty-five years from today. Please get busy.

(Signed) Board of Estimate.

And get busy you do, you and your fellow engineers!

The task set you does not come as a surprise. You have been making your own studies and you are prepared to go ahead without delay.

First, it is necessary to find a suitable watershed. A watershed is an area of land whose moisture drains into a stream or river or lake, or into an underground channel.

There are several musts to guide your choice of a watershed. Its water must be pure, of good color and odorless. It must have enough rain or snow to provide the required amount of water even in bad drought years. It must have a valley suitable for the construction of a dam to impound this water. It must be heavily wooded, because trees give off moisture and purify the air. It must be high enough above the level of the City to allow the water to flow down to the City without the expense of pumping. It must be as close to the City as possible, for every mile of aqueduct will cost over a million dollars.

Having chosen the watershed with the assistance of the United States Weather Bureau which has informed you about the rainfull, and a geologist who has helped you to decide into which stream most of that rainfall goes once it enters the soil, you proceed to plan a reservoir to collect the water of that stream.

The collecting reservoir will extend from a narrow point in the valley into which the stream flows to a very narrow point miles down on the stream, where it is possible to build a great wall or dam across the valley between the hills on either side. The dam will imprison the stream and keep it from carrying its water away. The water will pile up until it forms a vast lake. That is your reservoir.

Since the City is to pay for its new water system, it must, of course, know how much the job will cost. You therefore make a very careful record of all possible expenses. In forming the reservoir, it may well be that whole villages will be flooded under its waters, farms will be covered by it, railroad tracks and stations destroyed, roads drowned from sight.

The luckless inhabitants will have to be paid for the loss of their homes and businesses and farms and jobs. They will have to be helped, fairly, to begin life again elsewhere. Their cemeteries will have to be moved. Railroad tracks will have to be relocated and new highways built. Bridges may be needed. There will also be the costs of sewer systems which you will have to construct for towns and villages whose sewage would otherwise impair the purity of the water. All these costs must be included in your account.

Your dam, too, has certain musts. It must be powerful enough to resist the tremendous push of the imprisoned water. If the top of it is to be a highway, you must provide a lower wall or spillway that will permit flood waters to be carried off. Whichever is the spillway, whether the dam or the adjoining wall, it will have to be built in a series of steps on the waste side or else be provided with a pool at the bottom deep enough to break the fall of the water. There will also have to be a channel at the bottom of the spillway to carry the water off to a nearby stream.

Where the water from the reservoir is to enter the aqueduct, gates or valves must be provided by which the water can be shut out of the aqueduct or let in at any required rate. You will also need a building to house a laboratory, in which to test the water, and a chlorinating chamber to kill the impurities of the water as it enters the aqueduct.

Now for the aqueduct—the biggest part of the whole job. It will, of course, have to descend as it approaches the City. The usual grade is a drop of a little more than a foot in every mile. This is so the water will flow naturally and not have to be pumped.

You have first to decide whether the aqueduct is to be a grade tunnel blasted deep through the rock and then lined with concrete, or a grade tunnel built entirely of concrete and laid in a trench in the top earth.

If it is to be a rock tunnel, you take borings or samples of the rock to make sure that it will not cave into the tunnel while being dug and is solid enough to hold the great pressure of the water. This form of tunnel can be planned in a straight line from one end to the other. And as you know, a straight line is the shortest way between two points.

The tunnel will be built from shafts or holes sunk through the earth into the rock. These shafts may be between one and five miles apart. Men will go down these shafts and tunnel toward the next shaft without being an inch out of the way.

When the tunnel is completed some of these shafts will be closed at the bottom to keep the water from leaking out of the tunnel, and closed at the top to keep people and animals from falling in. Some will be used as riser shafts in which the water will rise to be piped at the top to neighboring communities. Some of them will contain powerful pumps able to empty sections of the aqueduct if at any time it were to need inspection or repair.

More riser shafts may be constructed to join the tunnel to an aqueduct crossing its path, so that, should either one of the tunnels be out of service, its waters could be carried on by the other. There may also be risers to connect the tunnel with the distribution reservoirs of other municipal systems which it passes. This is just in case either one of the systems should fail.

The second method of building an aqueduct is less expensive

and less dangerous than tunneling through rock. It is known as the cut-and-cover, because a shallow ditch is cut in the earth, the concrete aqueduct is laid in it, and the whole is covered by an embankment of earth. This aqueduct cannot go in a straight line. But neither is it to make too costly a curve around a hill. At some points you will find it cheaper to drive grade tunnels.

Both the cut-and-cover part of the aqueduct and the rock grade tunnels will be built horseshoe shape. The flowing water will pass 8 to 12 inches from the roof as it would between the banks of a stream. In this way, there will not be much pressure on the walls.

Where the cut-and-cover aqueduct encounters a swamp or a small valley, you may carry on with huge steel pipes; or, as in spanning the Narrows from Brooklyn to Staten Island, you may use cast iron pipes connected to each other by flexible joints. This form of construction is known as an inverted, or upside-down siphon.

Where the aqueduct must cross deep valleys or rivers, you will have to sink shafts on either side and blast the tunnel through the rock from shaft to shaft. The tunnel will be level and circular and lined with concrete. A very thin mortar will be shot through holes in the concrete wall in order to fill up all empty spaces between it and the rock. When in use, the tunnel will be entirely filled with water pressing powerfully against it. This is known as a pressure tunnel because the strength and weight of the rock all around it is great enough to keep the water from breaking through.

At intervals, whichever aqueduct you design must have meters to tell how much water is flowing through it. It must also have valves, which are really faucets, to control the flow or to shut it off entirely. Because on occasion it may be necessary to empty sections of the aqueduct, grade tunnels must be enabled to discharge into crossing streams while pressure tunnels must be provided with pumps powerful enough to dewater them.

Your next move is to plan a reservoir or several reservoirs in which to store enough water to supply the needs of the City should anything happen to cause the shutting off of the aqueduct up to that point. Whether the aqueduct is under the floor of the reservoir or above it, you will have to connect them by shafts and gates. You will also have to build a chamber for pumps to boost the water whenever it is required to move it from a lower level to a higher. This chamber is called a booster station.

Realizing that air and sunshine are great purifiers, you may decide to install an aerator at one of the reservoirs. If so, you will design a big basin close to the reservoir, containing hundreds of nozzles through which the water can be shot high into the air.

There is such an aerator at Ashokan Reservoir where the water jets into the sunshine in a gay and graceful curtain.

Leaving the storage reservoirs, your aqueduct now proceeds to the outer limits of the City. Here it will pass under or through an equalizing reservoir. You know, of course, that people use more water during the day than during the night and more water in the morning and evening than during any other part of the day. They also use more in very hot or very cold weather. The equalizing reservoir, which you will connect to the aqueduct by shafts and gates, is intended to supply the rush call for water. You will have to provide it with a testing laboratory and a chlorinating plant because, from that point on, the water is to enter the City to be used.

Now for the final and most important step. You have still to bring the water into the City. The best way to do so is to sink a shaft from the equalizing reservoir down into deep rock and begin tunneling. The reason for cutting the City tunnel sometimes as far as 700 feet under the street is to avoid injuring building foundations and subway tunnels and to make certain that the rock is strong enough to hold the billion gallons a day which is to rush through it, not for a day, or a year, but quite possibly for centuries.

Having plotted the entire course of this City pressure tunnel you indicate all the riser shafts which will be required to bring the water up to street level. These shafts will have to be topped by many valves or faucets opening into the mains which will distribute the water. Some of these shafts will be sunk at the same time as the shaft at the reservoir, so that many sections of the pressure tunnel can be blasted at the same time. You will also have to build a shaft which will permit the tunnel to be emptied into one of the City's rivers if it should have to be dewatered for purposes of inspection or repair.

If there is already a City water tunnel you will want to connect the new tunnel to it. One never knows what accidents may occur. If either tunnel needs to be closed off, New Yorkers need never know about it. The water will come through their faucets as if nothing were wrong.

Your tunnel, when completed, is designed to serve the people of four of the five boroughs that compose New York City, the Boroughs of the Bronx, Manhattan, Queens and Brooklyn. There remains the Borough of Richmond on Staten Island, whose population is also growing and will require more water.

You decide to lay a steel pipe main from one of the last of the riser shafts in Brooklyn to The Narrows. At this point Staten Island is about a mile across the water. The simplest way to span that distance is to construct a siphon that will drop down the Brooklyn bank, follow the bed of The Narrows, and climb up the bank of Staten Island. From there, it is quite easy to lay a steel pipe to Silver Lake Reservoir.

As with your reservoirs and aqueducts and City tunnels, you

connect the siphon to any other siphon which may have been built, so that at no point in the entire water system can a serious breakdown stop the service. Whatever happens, people must have water.

You may now draw a deep breath. The engineers on your Board of Water Supply have been working very hard. You take a look at the letter from the Board of Estimate. It is, perhaps, from two to five years old. What have you to show for that time?

You have not yet turned a handful of earth, but you have completed a working plan of the new water system. You know the source of the water and how much you can depend on. You know, by the borings of earth and rock, the substance of almost every foot through which the aqueduct will run. You know clearly how you will deliver the water to its final destination. And, very important, you have a good idea of the cost of the whole gigantic undertaking.

The next few steps do not depend upon you. The Board of Estimate must first approve your plans. Then the New York State Water Power and Control Commission must examine them to see that they are justified by public necessity, that they provide for safe and proper construction, that they do not injure the water supply of other state communities and that they are fair in their provision to pay all legal damages resulting to persons and property from the execution of the plans.

Having received the Commission's blessing, your plans and estimates of cost go back to the New York City Board of Estimate which must now raise the funds for construction by authorizing a loan to be made from the public.

The City is like a business. Every businessman must borrow money in order to carry on. So must the City. But as with the businessman, it cannot borrow above a certain total or limit. This limit is fixed by the New York State Constitution. However, the sums of money required to build New York City's water supply systems have been so immense that the City has been permitted to get them without regard to the borrowing limit. The public has been glad to lend the money both because of the importance of water supply and because the payments the City receives for the use of the water more than equal the huge costs of operation and interest on the loan.

You have not, of course, asked for the full amount of money

necessary to build the entire system. You can build only so much at a time. Each stage may take years. There is no sense in paying interest on money for which you have not as yet any use.

Granted the approval of the City Fathers and the money to go ahead, the Board of Water Supply now really clears the decks for action. Scores of new engineers and draftsmen are hired. The work of designing the first stage of the system is divided among you. As soon as the drawings of the various sections are completed, construction companies are invited to estimate the cost of building them. The lowest responsible bidder for each section will obtain the contract to go ahead.

Construction engineers in the pay of the Board will now join the contractors to see that the work and materials used are exactly as planned. Board inspectors will supervise the construction of camps and first-aid stations. A Board police force will see that order is maintained and that all sanitary rules are obeyed. This is no small task with perhaps twenty-five thousand men in the construction gangs.

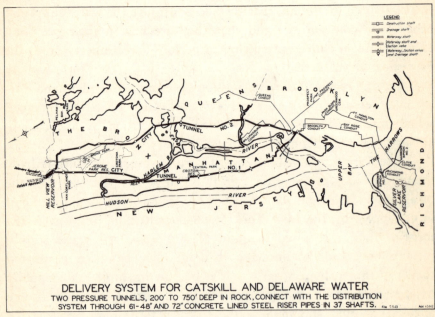

DELIVERY SYSTEM FOR CATSKILL AND DELAWARE WATER
TWO PRESSURE TUNNELS, 200' TO 750' DEEP IN ROCK, CONNECT WITH THE DISTRIBUTION
SYSTEM THROUGH 61-48" AND 72" CONCRETE LINED STEEL RISER PIPES IN 37 SHAFTS.

One day, somewhere along the line, a huge steam shovel will dig its teeth into the top soil—and the actual job of building a great city's water system will begin!

Six or eight or ten years later, a gate leading from a collecting reservoir opens into your new aqueduct. The imprisoned water pours into the tunnel. Good, clean, healthful, it courses along the smooth concrete walls, roars down the shafts leading to the pressure tunnels, again rises to the grade tunnel, dives down under the Hudson River, perhaps fifteen hundred feet, and finally enters the City tunnel. The riser shafts fill. The open valves lead the water into the huge distributing mains—and the first stage of your job is done! You have delivered the water.

The irony is that very few of the millions of people drinking the good water or taking a shower, or washing their sidewalks, will be aware of the nature of the modern miracle that has been created to serve them. We are all so prone to take for granted whatever exists.

New York City did not have a decent and plentiful supply of water until 1842 when its population numbered a third of a million. Imagine a city the size of Rochester, New York, or Portland, Oregon, depending on a few public and private wells and a private water works built to dispense only two gallons of water per person.

If you were to visit the Museum of the City of New York, you would see many beautifully made models showing stages in the history of the City. One of these models displays a scene at Bowling Green in 1831. The street is poorly cobbled. A gas lamp, one of the first in the City, is fixed to the garden fence. A gentleman is pushing by on a newfangled contraption, a bicycle without pedals. An omnibus drawn by four horses is being boarded by its passengers. At the rear of the scene is a big barrel on wheels, a water cart, making the daily rounds. Its water was probably drawn from the Tea Water Pump, the only good well in the City. Many people at that time depended mainly on rain water piped from their roofs into barrels or tanks.

Again and again, the city suffered attacks of typhoid, dysentery, cholera. The water was brackish and polluted. In 1828 a great fire destroyed several blocks because there was not enough water to fight it.

In 1829, the City erected the first public water works at Broadway and 13th Street. It consisted of a deep well from which the water was pumped into a cast iron tank. Two cast iron pipes bore the water from the tank into the City. The water was not good enough to drink. It was used only to fight fires. The wooden fire hydrants were equipped with padlocks so that no one could get to the water except the local fire fighting company.

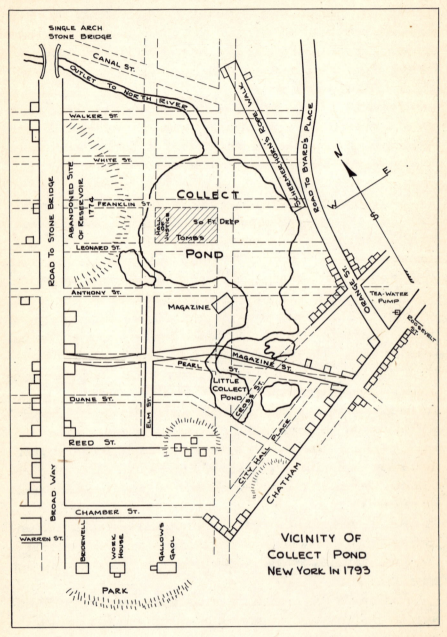

VICINITY OF
COLLECT POND
NEW YORK IN 1793

Finally the City Fathers were forced to consider the matter of an adequate public water supply. They decided to bring the water from Croton River, 32 miles above the City. In the winter of 1835, while they were still talking, occurred the most devastating fire the City had ever known. Six hundred and ninety-three houses and stores were destroyed. Thousands of people lost their homes and belongings. A desperate cry went up: Water! Water!

The City rushed its plans. It began the first Croton Aqueduct in 1837. On October 14, 1842, the entire population turned out to celebrate one of the most important events in two hundred years of the City's existence: the completion of a municipal system bringing to it a pure and abundant water supply.

As the City grew, it drew additional water from lakes and ponds in the Croton Watershed. By 1885, its one and a third million people needed more water than could pass through the Old Croton Aqueduct. The New Croton Aqueduct, as well as additional storage reservoirs were begun. A higher dam was built across the Croton River and in 1906 the old lake and dam were submerged under the new and larger lake. As in the case of the Old Croton Aqueduct, the water was distributed from reservoirs and gatehouses in the City.

But before this job could be completed the City was forced to begin planning an even larger water system. By 1898, the Bronx, Queens, and the City of Brooklyn had joined Manhattan to become part of the Greater City of New York with a combined population of three and a half million people. The Bronx had been served by private water companies drawing on the Bronx and Byram Rivers. Queens, Brooklyn and Richmond, or Staten Island, were also mostly served by private companies pumping their water from wells and cisterns. These boroughs had suffered whenever the rainfall of the year had been insufficient.

The City met its new problems by creating the Board of Water Supply in 1905. The Board set to work with will and imagination. It drew upon the Catskill Watershed. In 1917, it turned over the first stage of the immense Catskill System to the Department of Water Supply. The water was brought to the five boroughs by City Tunnel No. 1. The second stage of the undertaking was completed on January 1, 1928.

The City was now using almost nine hundred million gallons a day. Its population was seven million. But it was still growing.

Therefore, the Board of Water Supply began studying fresh sources of water supply long before the Catskill System was put into operation. It chose three new watersheds: Rondout Creek, draining into the Hudson River and the Neversink River and the East Branch of the Delaware draining into the Delaware River.

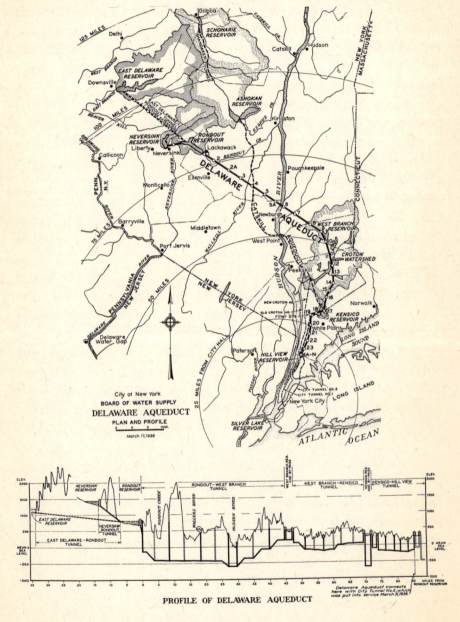

City of New York
BOARD OF WATER SUPPLY
DELAWARE AQUEDUCT
PLAN AND PROFILE
March 17, 1939

PROFILE OF DELAWARE AQUEDUCT

The State of New Jersey felt that the water of the whole Delaware River, even of the branches in New York State, was justly its own. However, the Supreme Court of the United States finally granted the City joint right to the watershed. Contractors began work on the Delaware Aqueduct early in 1937.

The first water of the Delaware System was brought into the City in 1946. The entire system will take many more years to complete and will add five hundred and forty million gallons a day to the billion gallons available before its construction.

Since the City uses about a billion gallons a day and since that is about all that City Tunnel No. 1 can carry, the Board of Water Supply built a second and much larger City tunnel in 1936. As you can see on the map, it too has a siphon to Staten Island. Remember that the City tunnels are joined and so are the siphons and the aqueducts. Nothing must interfere with the carriage of water. Water is life.

The Boroughs of Brooklyn, Queens and Richmond still use well water in addition to Catskill water. In some parts of Brooklyn and Queens this well water is supplied by private water companies who have to obey all the rules of the Department of Water Supply, Gas and Electricity.

This Department has one of the biggest all-time jobs in the

world. It maintains and operates the municipal water systems.
Its inspectors continually patrol the watersheds, the aqueduct lines
and the reservoirs to see that all are in order and that no sewage approaches them. Its chemists examine the water several times a day.
They treat it with chlorine. Sometimes, heavy rainstorms carry
particles of earth into the water. Then the chemists have to use

alum, a mineral salt, to force the earth particles to the bottom of the
reservoir.

Sometimes, sawbellys, tiny fish half an inch long, make the
thrilling journey from reservoir to faucet before they can be
screened out. Sometimes, algae, microscopic plants, find their way
into the water. They are not harmful, but they are disagreeable.
Some of this family make the water taste and smell fishy; others
give it a moldy, grassy taste; others make it taste like cucumbers;
and still others make one think of geraniums or even of candied
violets! The Department chemists soon get rid of this talented
family by rowing about the reservoir, trailing a porous bag of

copper sulphate in the water. The solution kills the algae and restores the natural taste of the water.

The Department is also a builder. After a system has been turned over to it, there are the great 72-inch trunk mains to be laid from the valves of the City tunnel shafts and the Croton gates to all points of distribution; there are the narrower mains that lead from the trunk mains to all the streets; and there are the pipe lines that lead from those mains to the house connections.

Mains and pipes are laid four feet under the street where the water will not freeze and where there will not be too much digging in case of emergency. Next time you go out in the streets, look for the covers over the valves of the mains and pipes.

Where the water must reach a hill too high for the natural flow of the water, the Department must build a pumping station. At certain high points, it must build equalizing storage tanks, called stand pipes. It provides the fire hydrants. In a later chapter we will see how in several sections of the City it has built special high pressure systems for the use of the fire fighters.

The Department of Water Supply does not pump water unless it has to. To pump a million gallons costs eighteen to twenty dollars.

The Department also saves millions of gallons a day by repairing underground leaks, by making public appeals to fix leaky faucets, and by placing water meters in all factories, office buildings and structures of other large users of water.

In 1930, we used 141 gallons a day per person. In 1938, we were using fifteen gallons less. We are still wasting a great deal of water. Still, we can congratulate ourselves. New Yorkers waste less water than the people of almost any other large American city. Chicago's users average 275 gallons a day. Detroit has an average of 160 gallons a day per person.

There are some men who still glorify war as an adventure. But peace is the greater adventure, a varied, constructive battle against all the foes of life. Look at the work we have just followed to completion. It required keen skill, honest team play, foresight, and tremendous courage and perseverance in the face of gigantic obstacles. And best of all, it brought whatever safety, health and joy exists in pure water.

Chapter 5

And Down The Drain

WHAT ARE SEWERS FOR? If you think this is a ridiculous question, consider the file of slaves that daily at evening bore buckets of human filth through New York to dump into the rivers. That was the picture in 1650, in 1750 and in 1850.

Not till Croton water reached the City did the more wealthy dwellers begin to build water closets that flushed into sewers. As late as 1900, there were still thousands of toilets which led to cesspools. Hundreds of humble men made a poor living, cleaning these cesspools and burying the contents.

Indeed, New York City's first sewers were simply gutter drains made of wood, then of stone and later of brick. Liquid kitchen slops were poured into the cesspools or out upon the ground. Garbage was thrown to the pigs and chickens in the street. It was thought that these wastes could do no harm. But storm water could flood cellars. Therefore, the householders built the sewers for one purpose only, to carry off the rains to the nearest stream.

By and by, a few citizens built drains from their kitchens to the cesspools and from the overflow of the cesspools to nearby streams. Thus the streams gradually became sewers.

Walk down to Broad Street. It has long been the financial heart of the country. At its Wall Street end is the U.S. Treasury flanked by the House of Morgan on the left and the New York Stock Exchange on the right. But Broad Street began as a brook. The Dutch, homesick for Holland, widened it into a canal. In 1680, the English governor covered the canal with a roadway and it became the City's first "common seuer." If Broad Street could write its own story, it might well call it, "How I Got Rich Though Born in a Ditch."

In 1819, five years after the canal through Canal Street was completed, an open stone sewer was laid alongside it. Strangely enough, the sewer did not prevent the leafy road becoming one of the most fashionable strolling places in the City.

By the time the Croton water poured through the aqueduct, two more stone sewers had been constructed. But the soil and wells of the City had long ago become poisoned by the leaking cesspools. The people had already been through several severe plagues.

Now, given a marvelous abundance of water, some people began building water closets in their homes. The sewers had a new use for which they had not been designed. Foul odors rose out of them. The authorities did their best to sweeten the stench but neglected the cause. The sewers clogged. Heavy rains washed their contents into the street and spread disease. Citizens complained bitterly.

But, as you may remember, sanitation was scarcely better anywhere else in the world. England was quite alarmed at its own vile, plaguey state. It appointed a body of men to investigate causes and find remedies.

Along with the rest of the Western world, New York City studied the historic report made by England's Health of Towns Commission. As a result, the Common Council began earnestly building sewers, though without any definite plan. It built them larger. It changed their materials from stone to brick to hard-fired or vitreous clay pipes through which the sewage could flow more smoothly. It changed the shape of sewers from round to oval and back again, hoping to effect a deeper, swifter flow. Its task seemed solely to provide sewers as rapidly as the fast growing City expanded.

This it did without realizing that while it was solving one problem, it was creating another.

All the sewers emptied into the water surrounding New York City. As cesspools gave way to water closets draining into the sewers, the condition of the rivers and harbor and beaches became unpleasant. Not until the 1890's, however, when the waters were unsightly and stank mightily, did anyone realize that it was no longer enough to build sewers. It had now become necessary to clean the sewage of its putrid, germ-laden matter before allowing it to enter the surrounding waters.

The City of Brooklyn was the first in the United States to treat its sewage. Its beaches in Coney Island had become foul. Often, bathers came away with skin rashes. Those who swallowed the water were often ill afterwards. Some of them died of the poisoning.

Brooklyn, thereupon, built several small plants in Coney Island in which the solid matter in the sewage had a chance to settle to the bottom of tanks. A portion of lime or ferric chloride was used to speed the settling. The solid matter, or, as the sanitation men call it, the sludge, was then removed and buried. The liquid sewage was further treated with chlorine before it entered the ocean.

Despite this brave beginning, it was not until 1931 that New York City had a plan for the construction of sewage treatment plants. This plan was made by the one-year-old Department of Sanitation.

In the forty years since Brooklyn had shown the way, the City had managed to build a few more small plants in which the sludge was screened out. But all these plants together removed only about one per cent of the sludge of the City sewage. The Boroughs continued to build sewers that emptied into the nearest waters.

The Department of Sanitation not only planned, it actually went to work on the plan. In 1935, it completed and put in operation two enormous projects, the Coney Island Sewage Treatment Works and the Ward's Island Sewage Treatment Works.

In 1938, the Department of Public Works took over the responsibility for carrying out the rest of the program. The next year it put into operation the Tallman's Island Sewage Treatment Works in time to service New York City's World's Fair. It hopes to complete construction to treat all the sewage of the City by 1950.

Before we have a look at how sewage is treated, we had better make sure that we know what sewage is. Sewage is the discarded water of a community after it has been polluted by all sorts of waste matter from sinks, toilets and work places. The dirt washed from the streets by rain and street flushing is also a part of it.

The sewage from buildings leaves through six-inch pipes that connect with the street sewer. The street sewer is a combination sanitary and storm sewer, usually made of vitrified pipe, twelve inches or more in diameter. It is laid eight to twelve feet below street level. If the street sewer is larger than twenty-four inches it is made of cement or brick. Its sewage flows into a concrete collecting sewer that is usually five feet or more in diameter. It is these collecting sewers which emptied into the City waters before the treatment works were built.

Surprisingly enough, all the solids in sewage amount to no more than a spoonful in a big barrel of water. And yet, because New York City's sewage, like its water supply, is about a billion gallons a day, it contains about one thousand tons of solids. These solids must be removed and the harmful bacteria destroyed, if our surrounding waters are not to be offensive, destructive of marine life, dangerous to bathers and harmful to everyone's health.

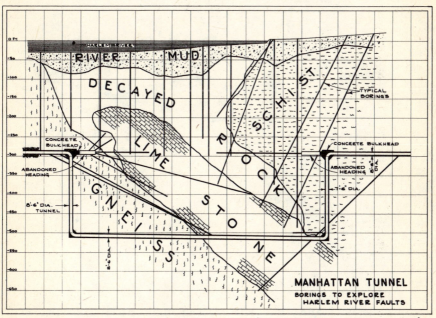

The sewage plan divides the five Boroughs into seventeen draining areas, each sloping toward a water way. Each of these districts is to have a great master sewer, called an intercepting sewer, which will receive the flow of the collecting sewers and deliver it at its own district treatment plant.

A glance at the map will show you that the intercepting sewers follow the banks of the City. That is because they must be built at a point lower than the collecting sewers in order to permit gravity flow. All sewers today are built at downgrades sufficient to speed the sewage through at the rate of at least two or three feet per second. Thus the new sewers are self-cleansing.

At this writing, the City has three methods of treating its sewage. That is because the science of sewage treatment is still so young that it is experimental. In fact, the engineers of the Bureau of Sewage Disposal whose business it is to design the remaining treatment plants, hesitate to say what these plants will be like. They are still testing and improving their knowledge and eagerly searching for better and cheaper processing methods.

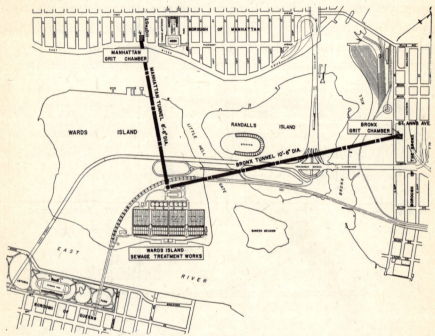

Another reason for differing methods is that sewage differs in various districts and that one district may need fifty per cent cleaning while another may need close to ninety per cent. It is believed that the oxygen in the ocean and in the rivers can take care of what impurities remain.

New York City is to have no new screening plants, but screening is one of the methods it uses. By far the most unique of this type of plant is the one at the extreme western end of Canal Street. It is completely underground and for the most part below water level. The intercepting sewer pours its wastes through iron crossbars which catch all the big matter in the sewage. The sewage then enters two deep cement tanks, through which it flows very slowly. At the further end of each tank is a wall high enough to stop the low floating grit from going further and low enough to permit the sewage to go on through a channel to the two screens. An air suction pump blows the gathered grit into a hopper from which it is later pumped into a tank truck which hauls it away.

The Canal Street screen is really an endless belt of copper screens traveling on a steep incline. It is the only one of its kind in the country. Screens at the other plants are simply large circular sieves. At its low end, the belt screen picks up the sludge in the passing sewage, carries it upward to give it a chance to drain and then at the top, shifts it into a hopper. As the screen plates go under and down again, a line of brushes sweeps against them and a sharp spray of water washes them clean.

The remaining sewage, called the effluent, flows into a well from which it is pumped into the Hudson River. The sludge is carted away to an incinerator and burned.

The process at the Coney Island Treatment Works also begins with the removal of grit. From the grit chamber, the sewage enters the sedimentation tanks, taking two hours to flow through them to the point where it is chlorinated and pumped into the ocean. Ferric chloride sulphate helps settle the sludge to the bottom of the sedimentation tanks. The sludge is then pumped into what are called digester tanks.

There, kept at a hot summer temperature for sixty days, the sludge rots and breaks up. One of the results of this period of breakup is methane gas which rises to the top and is piped away to a storage point. The gas is used to operate three 900-horsepower gas engines which drive the electric generators that furnish all the light, heat and power used in the plant.

Large quantities of the digested sludge are being used as fertilizer in the City parks.

The Ward's Island plant uses the activated sludge process.

Before the Bronx intercepting tunnel crosses the river to Ward's Island, its sewage passes through grit chambers slowly enough to allow most of the grit and heavy solids to settle to the bottom. The grit is then pumped into a hopper and trucked away to one of the many undeveloped lowlands which the Department of Sanitation is constantly filling in.

Crossing the river, the tunnels bring the sewage to the preliminary settling tanks. The sewage takes an hour to flow through one of these tanks, leaving behind about half its sludge content. This raw sludge is then pumped directly to the storage building at the dock.

Continuing its flow, the remaining sewage enters sixteen aeration tanks. This is where the activating process takes place. Air is forced upward through slabs of earthenware or of carborundum, at the bottom of the aeration tanks. As it comes out the other side of the slab, the stream is divided into hundreds of fine jets. The air does two things as it boils upward. It enlivens or activates the good oxygen breathing bacteria which thereupon destroy the dangerous bacteria. It also causes the filth to floc together in solid lumps. This process takes five hours.

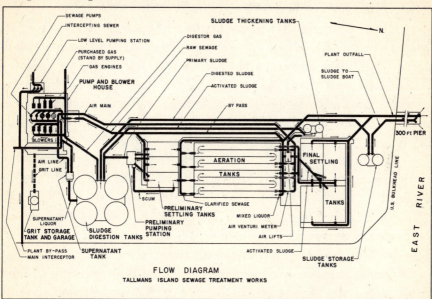

FLOW DIAGRAM
TALLMANS ISLAND SEWAGE TREATMENT WORKS

The sewage from each aeration tank, continuing its flow, now enters two final settling tanks for a two-and-a-half hour stay. Here the floc settles out. Because it is now full of activated bacteria, most of the floc is pumped back to the aeration tanks to help lick the harmful bacteria in the new batch of sewage into a harmless state. The rest of the sludge is pumped to the storage building at the dock. It still has forty times as much water as solids.

Here it is loaded on three specially built steel sludge vessels, which then proceed to a point in the ocean ten miles from the nearest land. The sludge is pumped out and, being heavier than water, settles to the bottom of the sea.

The Tallman's Island Treatment Works uses the activated sludge process and then digests the sludge and feeds the resulting gas back to itself as light, heat and power. The digested sludge is taken away by one of the sludge vessels.

All sewage works are operated and maintained by the Department of Public Works.

The forward strides the City has made in its sewage picture are at once apparent if you look at it this way. Of the one thousand tons of sludge in the day's sewage, it removed ten tons in 1934 and four hundred and fifty tons in 1940. By 1950 it hopes to have sufficient plants to treat an expected one and a half billion gallons a day of sewage.

It may be, then, that all the plants will generate their own light, heat and power. There are some communities in Europe which actually sell this power to their citizens. Certainly the digested sludge can help many a farmer raise a good crop. Milwaukee markets its sludge as fertilizer. Other new and important uses may be found for it. Even perfumes and drugs may be made of sludge.

One thing is certain: New York City is rapidly on the way to becoming one of the cleanest and healthiest of the world's great cities.

For this, the Department of Sanitation too deserves great praise. Its broom sweeps from our streets half a million tons of trash a year. Hundreds of flushing machines wash the streets free of dust. Best of all, garbage is no longer scowed to sea and dumped only to float back to our shores. It is now burned in the modern incinerators built for that purpose or used as a sanitary land fill.

Yes, the Department of Public Works, the Department of Sanitation and the Department of Health are doing an important job well. But, of course, it is our City. We can help keep it clean and healthful.

The Department of Sanitation once had a Junior Inspectors' Club, one hundred and sixty thousand strong. Today, it invites boys and girls between the ages of six and eighteen to join the Clean City League clubs in their schools or to form such clubs if they do not already exist. The heads of the clubs wear gold badges, their deputies wear silver badges. But it isn't the badges that are fun. It is the talks with members of the Department, the booklets, the movies, the discussions with the Commissioner of the serious problems of sanitation, the visits to incinerators and landfills. And with the fun goes the responsibility of helping the Department keep your own neighborhood clean in accordance with the slogan for all of us: *Keep The City Clean!*

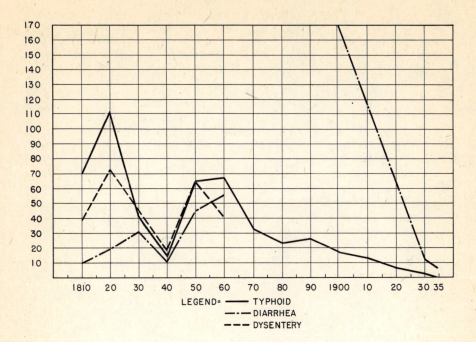

LEGEND= ——— TYPHOID
        —·—·— DIARRHEA
        ——— DYSENTERY

# PART III
# ENERGY

## Chapter 6

## City Without Chimneys

HAVING PROVIDED THE CITY with water and sewers, we have now to equip it with heat for warmth and for cooking, with light that will continue day into the night, and with power for transportation, for communication and for work. In other words, we must set up the machinery for the three great energies of our Power Age: Steam, Gas and Electricity.

Of these, steam is a graybeard of some two hundred years, gas is over a century old, and electricity is a mere youngster of sixty-five. Their enormous capacity for work ended the age of handicrafts and brought in its stead the Industrial Machine Age.

Gradually, the Feudal System crumbled. Peasants, often forced off their land, flocked to the city factories. Merchants and factory owners grew in number and in power. When they rebelled against the tyranny of kings and lords, the workers fought with them for a new freedom. That is how Democracy was born. To a great extent it was a child of steam.

But how could steam help create a revolution? The answer is that steam itself was a revolution in man's everyday life.

For tens of thousands of years, his power was confined to his own muscles. One tenth of a horse power, or, as the engineers write it, $\frac{1}{10}$ h. p., was the most that he could produce. The teaming up of slaves to push a wheel or to drive a galley multiplied that power. The invention of the lever helped a great deal.

Then somewhere along the curve of time, man acquired an energy outside of his own muscles. He domesticated the dog, the horse, the camel, the elephant, the donkey, the mule and the ox.

One day, quite recently in fact, only five or six thousand years ago, he accidentally discovered the sail, father of the windmill. It was his first step in mechanical power and in harnessing the tremendous forces of nature. By and by, he learned to tap the power of water, thrusting the teeth of his water wheel into its onrush.

Not until the end of the Sixteenth Century was he able to glimpse the possibilities of producing an artificial power. That power was steam.

We have all read the inspiring story in which little James Watt, watching his mother's tea kettle, becomes the first to discover the power of steam. The fact is that this discovery had been made at least as far back as the Second Century B. C., when Hero of Alexandria constructed a toy rotary steam engine. For seventeen centuries, however, the great giant Steam was permitted to slumber on, being awakened only to serve in the mysterious opening of temple doors.

Then, in about 1570, men began to experiment with the expanding energy that rises from boiling water. At first they used it as power for church organs or for forcing water into fountain play. But little by little they learned how to harness it for work.

In 1702, Captain Thomas Savery of England built the first steam engine. It was used to pump water out of a coal mine. It wasn't very good. But along came Thomas Newcomen, a blacksmith, who improved on Savery, and James Watt who improved on Newcomen. By 1780, England was "steam-mill mad." London, Manchester, Birmingham were becoming big factory towns. With the invention of the steam locomotive, the Steam Age arrived!

A work engine developing 5,000 h. p., was equal in power to 50,000 men; an engine of 25,000 h. p., equalled the power of 250,000 men. Man developed undreamed speeds in the production of goods and in travel by land and sea. Is it any wonder, then, that as he began freeing himself from the slow, laborious handicraft days he should, at the same time, have rebelled against the restraints of feudal kingdoms? So, as you see, steam was responsible for more than one kind of revolution.

Today, steam is still one of our most important energies. But it is not out where we can see it easily. Time was when the trains that roared in and out of New York City devoured wood and coal and spat cinders; when the cars on our Els were pulled by engines belching flame and smoke; when automobiles were powered by fire and water; when fire engines were fire-eaters; when streets were dug by whistling tools; when factories ran their machinery by steam.

But steam is no longer a direct mover. It has been replaced by the gasoline engine, the diesel oil engine and, above all, by the electric motor. Today, it is the power behind the scenes. Its mighty turbines, some having 200,000 h. p., or the energy of two million slaves, whirl the electric generators which manufacture our electric power. Its eight-story boilers generate the white energy that charges hotly under Manhattan streets into the skyscrapers and into most of the hotels, theaters, apartment houses, factories, department stores and wealthier homes from the Battery to 92nd Street.

Most of us, when we think of steam, think of it as a house warmer. And yet, its domestic history is less than one hundred years old. True, James Watt had warmed his writing room with an iron steam box, probably the first steam radiator. But steam heating did not come noticeably into use until after the Civil War.

Most of the apartment houses in New York City built before 1914 were once equipped with coal stoves in every kitchen. The largest percentage of these did not install steam heating systems until after World War I. There are still many apartments in which the coal stove is winter king.

I lived in just such "cold flats" until 1920. We stored the coal in one of the many bins in the basement of the tenement. In cold weather, it was my duty to carry the ashes to the street and bring up several buckets of coal. Imagine your own street in those days. Instead of a few deliveries of coal, there were as many as there were tenants. The waste was terrific, the smoke dense and full of soot, and the sidewalks dirty with uncollected ashes often exposed to the wind.

The gradual introduction of steam heat changed all that.

The most important development, however, was the production of steam at a central plant and its distribution by pipe line to many buildings. Birdsill Holly is the man who proved that it was possible by constructing just such a system in his home town, Lockport, New York. A few years later, in 1881, The New York Steam Company began building a central heating system in lower Manhattan.

How curious that steam should have become a public utility at the same time that electricity was making its first commercial bow! Let us listen to Thomas Edison tell about the time when he and the steam engineer, big Charles Emery, were nursing their babies along.

"While I was digging the trenches and putting in the tubes

in several miles of street in the First District, The New York Steam Company was also digging trenches and putting in steam heating pipes. Mr. C. E. Emery, then chief engineer, and I would meet quite frequently at all hours of the night, I looking after my tubes and he after his pipes. At the same time that Emery was putting down his pipes, another concern started in opposition to The New York Steam Company and was also working nights putting down its pipes in Maiden Lane. I used to talk to Emery about the success of his scheme.

"I thought he had a harder proposition than I had, and he thought that mine was harder than his. But one thing we both agreed on, and that was the other steam heating engineer hadn't any chances at all, and that his company would surely fail. If he, Emery, was right the other fellow was wrong. Emery used mineral wool to surround his pipes, which was of a fibrous nature and was stuffed in boxes to prevent loss of heat and pressure, whereas his competitor was laying his pipes in square boxes filled with lampblack.

"Before Emery had finished all his pipes and was working in the street one night, he heard a terrible rush of steam. It seems his competitor had put on steam pressure to test out his pipes. There was a leak in the pipe; the steam got into the lampblack and blew up, throwing three tons of lampblack all over the place, and covering fronts of several stores in Maiden Lane. When the people came down the next morning, everything was covered with lampblack—and the company 'busted'!"

Evidently, the problems arising from the construction of a central heating system were not easy to solve. However, Emery did find the right answers. Indeed, he built so well that some of his pipe is still on the job.

For the first time in the recorded history of the Temperate Zone, architects began erecting buildings without chimneys. They employed the valuable boiler space for vaults and stores and workshops and dining rooms. They ripped the boilers out of old structures and put the space to profitable use. It was cheaper and cleaner to buy steam than to make it.

Today, The New York Steam Corporation supplies steam to about one-seventh of the total building volume in Manhattan. One-third of the supply is used for hot water, cooking, laundry, refrigeration and for scores of industrial purposes.

The Steam Corporation has four plants situated on the East River. The largest of these, and the largest central station steam plant in the world, is the Kips Bay Station at East 35th Street. This station has a capacity of almost two and a half million pounds of steam an hour. The other three stations together can generate a like amount. In addition, the corporation can draw a total of about two million pounds per hour from the Waterside and 14th Street Stations of its powerful parent, the Consolidated Edison Company. It also has available approximately 850,000 pounds per hour in rented generating capacity. All together, its output on a generated basis is about 7,850,000 pounds of steam an hour.

Briefly, the process starts with the coal brought to the station by barges. The coal is swung up to the top of the plant and dropped into the raw coal bunker. From there it is fed to the giant pulverizers which crush it into a fine powder that will burn with the least waste, almost like a gas. The powdered coal is then blown into a cyclone in which the air is separated from the coal. The coal dust is now pumped into bins on either side of the boiler. From these bins it is fed automatically into the furnace of the boiler.

The air necessary for maintaining combustion, is mechanically sucked in from the outside at the top of the building. It is then forced into heaters that raise it to a temperature of 367° F. From the heaters it is blown into the furnace.

In spite of the terrific heats generated in the furnace and the boiler, this structure is so well insulated and water-cooled that practically no heat escapes outside its walls.

The ashes drop into the pits below the furnace. The flying cinders and soot are precipitated just before the smoke enters the great chimneys. These wastes are wetted down and removed by barge or truck.

The water in the boiler comes from the City mains. Chemicals are added to it to prevent dissolved substances in it from leaving a scale on the boiler walls or the entering mains. On its way to the top of the boiler, the water is heated until, by the time it enters the boiler, its temperature is over 300° F. It is converted almost at once into live, compressed steam having a pressure of 285 pounds per square inch. This pressure has to be tamed down to between 130 and 175 pounds before it can be allowed to enter the distributing mains in the street.

The distributing mains, laid between 4 and 15 feet deep, interconnect under the streets like a gridiron so that any one of the generating stations can transmit its load through the entire system. The mains are generously supplied with valves which can be used to send a heavier load of steam in any required direction. They are made of welded steel capable of resisting 250 pounds pressure per square inch. The sections are joined together at intervals by copper joints which permit sufficient expansion to keep the pipes from buckling. In case of trouble or necessary changes, they can be reached through frequent manholes.

At strategic points, pressure gauges record the rise and fall of consumer use and transmit the story to the electric control dials at the station. Thus the engineers know how much steam is being used and how much they must supply.

Leaving the distributing mains, the steam sizzles into the

service pipes which lead it directly into the consumers' buildings. Here it is metered as used. The rates, as in gas or electricity, vary with the amount used.

Whether it enters a private residence or spurts into the 1252 foot shaft of the Empire State Building, steam does its job equally well. In one place it will humbly press suits and block hats. In another, it will supply hot water for a big laundry. It will do the cooking and the washing in a "Coffee Pot" or in a swanky hotel restaurant, and then get on the outside of the hotel and steam its walls as clean as the day its doors were first opened. It will heat a barber's towel and at the same time do an excellent job as assistant in a dye house or a tannery. It will supply the scorching fog in a turkish bath and then proceed to the Metropolitan Opera House where it may be called upon to issue from the nostrils of an enraged dragon or burst terrifyingly from the very pit of Hell.

Some day, no doubt, all civilized communities will be centrally heated whether by steam, electricity, or atomic energy. In that day, you will find it difficult to explain to your children or grandchildren why it was not possible to do so sooner; why precious coal had to be wasted in tiny individual furnaces; why your generation had to put up with coal trucks, ash cans and ash-collecting trucks; and why you had to suffer the insanitary nuisance of thousands of small, inefficient chimneys each polluting the air.

You will, however, find some measure of satisfaction in having lived through and perhaps contributed to the change. It will have happened in your lifetime just as most of the progress that has already taken place has happened in your grandfather's and father's lifetime.

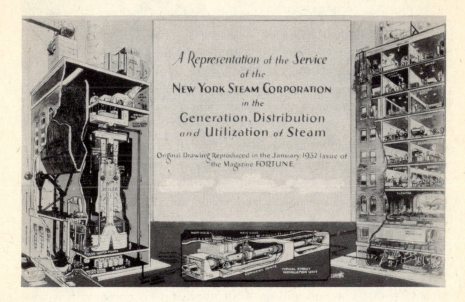

## Chapter 7

## Chaos Into Gas

"THERE'S A MADMAN PROPOSING to light London with—what do you think? Why, with smoke!" cried Sir Walter Scott contemptuously.

"Gas? What foolishness!" sneered Napoleon as he marched on toward the folly of the Russian invasion.

"A sin!" cried some. "Gas will make night into day. This, the Lord never intended."

"The City Beautiful, that is what gas will make of London!" So spoke Frederick Albert Winsor, the "madman" who had angered Scott by lighting Pall Mall, one of the city's famous thoroughfares.

Five years later, in 1812, Winsor's gas company, the first in the world, began in earnest to light the streets of London.

Paris followed suit in 1820.

In the New World, Rembrandt Peale, of Baltimore, an artist who had painted George Washington, illuminated his museum with gas. That same year, 1816, he received a charter to manufacture gas, to lay pipes and to light the streets of Baltimore.

The age of whale oil lamps and the long centuries of wax and tallow dip candles were doomed. The whalers and the chandlers did their best to stop cities from granting charters to gas companies. But though progress may be delayed, it cannot be stopped.

All over the world, city after city began lighting its streets with what, in 1609, Jean Baptiste van Helmont of Brussels had named "gas."

Physician, chemist and alchemist, van Helmont, while searching for the secret that would turn base materials into gold, recognized that the fuels which he burned under his cauldrons, gave off, besides smoke, an invisible "wild spirit" or, in Greek, *chaos*. He called it "gas."

For two hundred years following van Helmont, scientists struggled to harness gas and to put it to work. Finally, in 1792, William Murdock, the inventor of the locomotive, succeeded in freeing the gas in coal, piping it and lighting his home with it.

In the one hundred and fifty years since, van Helmont's "chaos" has grown up to do a most important job. It is now producing billions of units of energy. It not only does our cooking and heats many of our homes, it is used in the manufacture of glass, tile, metals, rubber, varnish, coins, books. Its energy melts, hardens, freezes, tempers, colors and shapes. It is one of the greatest miracle workers in an age of miracles.

The fact is that van Helmont had discovered the secret of immense wealth. He had been successful in his search—and had not known it!

Gas had a hard struggle on its way up to our century. At first it had to fight the complaints of the ignorant and superstitious. Then the whale oil and candle people went after it. Not until the Civil War was over, did it begin the lighting of homes on a large scale. Then just as its future seemed bright, kerosene lamps were introduced. Oil lamps were greatly improved. And both gave more light than the gas of that period.

The young industry was in despair. But soon two men came to its assistance. Tessie du Motay, working in France, and Thaddeus S. C. Lowe, working in America, invented a new process of manufacturing gas. They called the process "water gas."

The new process added so much candle power to gas, that it once more shot ahead of all other illuminating fuels. People now not only preferred it for lighting, they began to use it for cooking. The first gas stoves were imported from England. And just as the gas industry seemed to face a most profitable future—along came Edison and electric lighting!

Now the industry seemed truly doomed. It fought back by inventing the gas mantle, a fixture which gave a bright white light. But all the time it knew that its days as a lighting agent were numbered. It therefore began diligently to explore other fields in which it might be useful. Lower rates allowed its product to enter more and more homes as a cooking fuel. It kept pace with the tremendous development of industry and discovered thousands of uses for gas and its by-products. Today, gas is one of man's most valuable servants.

New York City did not begin gas lighting its streets until 1828. Starting in 1697, every seventh householder was required to hang a lamp out of his second-story window. The law excused him on moonlit nights. No wonder people seldom went out after dark. In 1762 oil lamps were first lighted on the sidewalks.

In 1816, the City had set up a small experimental gas plant at one of the northern corners of City Hall Park. The gas was distilled from rosin and was conveyed by tin pipes up Chatham Street and down Broadway to Fulton Street. But though pedestrians and shopkeepers were highly pleased with its brilliant effect, the whalers and candle makers forced the City to abandon the experiment.

Finally, in 1823, Samuel Leggett, whose home at 7 Cherry Street was the first in the City to be gas lit, obtained a charter to go ahead. He formed the New York Gas Light Company. Off to London went Timothy Dewey, the superintendent, in order to learn the newest methods of manufacture, to buy all the necessary fixtures and to hire men who knew how to set them up.

The plant was built at what is now Hester and Centre Streets.

On February 14, 1825, the ovens were fired and a new energy, gas made of oil, was put at the service of New Yorkers. A few years later, the Hester Street plant stopped using oil and changed to rosin.

As the City expanded, more and more gas companies came into being. They used different processes and constantly quarrelled and fought among themselves. The result was costly. In 1860, they sold gas at $2.50 for one thousand cubic feet. The industry could not grow while rates were so high.

Then, frightened by the development of the kerosene lamp as well as by the wastefulness of the fierce competition among themselves, they formed, in 1884, a single company, the Consolidated Gas Company of New York. The new Company went ahead so fast that by 1900 it had brought the price of gas down to $1.05 for one thousand cubic feet. By 1910, the rate was down to $.80. The old iron coal stove was now rapidly giving way to the gas range. Today, only a few of those apartments that still use coal stoves for heating do not have gas ranges.

There are two kinds of gas, natural gas and manufactured

gas. Natural gas was known to the ancients, some of whom saw it as a column of flame to fear and worship, while others used it to evaporate salt. It is found in wells in coal and oil regions and is piped to points of use, sometimes hundreds of miles away. Manufactured gas is made from bituminous coal and from coke and oil. In New York City, gas is made from coal and coke. Coal gas is made in coke ovens, the process resulting in both gas and coke. It is this coke that is used in the carburetted water gas process which Lowe invented.

Would you like to make coke oven gas? Fill the bowl of a clay pipe with small fragments of bituminous coal, paste clay over the top and place the bowl in a hot fire. You will see that smoke begins to issue from the stem. This smoke is gas. You can light it. With the gas will come a black tarry liquid. This is the impurity in the gas. When the gas light goes out, remove the clay top. Instead of coal, you will now find coke. Simple, isn't it?

Of course, the commercial process is more complicated. When possible, gas plants are situated at waterside. There are several reasons for this: gas must be cooled and quantities of water are required for economical cooling; a waterway permits coal and oil to be barged to the plant; since gas rises, it is best to build the plant at water level, which is usually the lowest point in the community, and thus save pumping costs.

When ready to be used, the coal is ground to the fineness of powder and fed into the great coke ovens, thirteen tons to an oven. These ovens are red-hot. They are grouped together, 3 to 9 of them forming one group or bench.

At first, the coal becomes plastic. But soon it begins to bubble and boil and throw off gas. The gas rises to the top of the oven and passes into a main that collects the gases of the entire bench. After fourteen hours of heating, the gas has been driven off and what remains is coke. This is removed and a fresh charge of coal immediately takes its place. The ovens are never allowed to cool.

What we have now besides the coke is a crude impure gas. You recall the tarry liquid that leaked out of your clay pipe? It is necessary to cool and scrub—yes, scrub the crude gas before it can be sent on its thousands of tasks.

The collecting main is half full of water. As the hot gas passes through it, some of the tar is caught and held by the water. The gas is then sucked down to the bottom of a tower known as a Primary Cooler. As it rises to the top, trays of cooled ammonia liquor take some of the heat out of it.

It is now forced into another cylindrical shell with tiny holes set in its bell-shaped metal top. As the gas strikes this top, it leaves some of its tar on the surface of the metal before it can escape through the holes. Once more it encounters a perforated metal ceiling. The speed of its flow, and the change of direction which it is forced to take in order to escape through the new holes, comb it of all tar. Another method uses electric charges that knock the tar out of the gas.

But it is not yet pure enough to use efficiently. It has a certain amount of ammonia that must be washed out. It is therefore reheated in a steel tank containing steam pipes and passed into a lead-lined tank holding a weak solution of sulphuric acid. The gas enters at the bottom of this tank, or Saturator, and bubbles to the top, leaving behind it tiny crystals of ammonium sulphate.

The gas is then cleaned of any acid it may still contain and passes into the Final Cooler. Here, finely sprayed river water brings its temperature down to what it will be when it enters our homes.

The naphthalene scrubbers now go to work on the gas, spraying a light oil down upon it and freeing it of naphthalene. At this point, only one impurity remains in the gas: hydrogen sulphide. This is removed when the gas passes through the Purifiers, large steel boxes containing several layers of wooden trays covered with oxide of iron mixed with wood shavings. The oxide of iron attracts and holds the hydrogen sulphide. Every six months the box is exposed to the air, whereupon the oxide of iron is returned to its former state.

The gas is at last ready to use. It has been cleansed of tar, coke dust, pitch, water vapor, ammonia, naphthalene and hydrogen sulphide. It now passes through a meter which measures it and then into the great storage holders.

But still it is not sent out on its many tasks. The Public Service Commission of the State of New York requires that gas contain 537 British thermal units per thousand cubic feet. A British thermal unit is a measurement of heat sufficient to raise the temperature of water one degree Fahrenheit per pound of water. But coke oven gas does not contain the required thermal units. Therefore, it must be pepped up with an enriched gas. That enriched gas is carburetted water gas.

Water gas is made in an apparatus consisting of three cylindrical shells joined together and lined with heat-resisting blocks made of brick and silica. The first cylinder is the generator. Into it go about two tons of the coke made in the coke ovens. After ignition a blast of air is blown into it raising the coke to a white hot glow. The hot gases pass through the other two cylinders and out into the air.

When the three cylinders of the water gas set are sufficiently hot, the air is shut off and steam is forced into the generator up through the bed of coke. The terrific heat breaks up the steam into hydrogen gas particles which unite with the coke gas to form blue water gas.

This gas as it leaves the generator has a low heating value. It needs to be pepped up or carburetted. It therefore passes into the next cylinder which is the carburetter. This cylinder is built like a honeycomb of fired brick. Very fine sprays of gas oil are shot into it from the top. As the oil strikes the hot bricks, it breaks up into the gas which mixes with the water gas. The oil gas is the carburetter. It is what peps up the water gas to the required heat value.

The mixture of the two now passes into the last cylinder, the superheater. The superheater is also built of honeycombed fired brick. The intense heat given off by its glowing bricks welds or fixes the carburetted water gas so that it will not separate.

The period during which air is forced into the generator is called the "blow." The gas-making period is called the "run." Since the run cools the water gas set, there has to be a blow between each run to reheat the set. The generator takes a new charge of coke every thirty minutes.

The carburetted water gas goes through much the same purifying process as the coke oven gas.

A mixture of these two gases is the gas we burn.

The coke ovens are heated by producer gas, which is made by blowing air through a coke fire. It is not purified. It simply passes through a water bath which removes its dust. The amount of producer gas a plant uses is about equal to the amount of coke oven gas it manufactures.

The largest single structures in a gas plant are the steel gas tanks or holders in which the commercial gas is stored. From these holders the gas passes to the district holders and so finally to the consumers.

Perhaps you have sometimes wondered what prevents these huge tanks, some of them storing fifteen million cubic feet of inflammable gas, from exploding? The answer is that an explosion needs air. There is no air in a holder.

The type of holder we most generally see is known as a water-sealed holder and is based on the principle discovered in 1781 by Lavoisier, a great French chemist. You know what a collapsible aluminum cup is? If you were to set it mouth down, its upper sections would collapse into the lowest. If, then, you were to blow gas into it, these sections would be forced to rise and make room for the gas. That is the idea of a water-sealed holder. Its lowest section is largely full of water to prevent the gas from leaking into the ground. The sections move on rails and the spaces between them are protected against leakage by water seals.

A newer type of gas holder is waterless and is rigid. Under its roof is a ceiling on a moving piston which rises and falls with the amount of gas in the holder.

The weight of the sections in the water-sealed holder and the weight of the ceiling in the waterless holder force the gas on its way

into the mains.   Nevertheless, holder stations are generally equipped
with pumps.   These pumps can both blow and exhaust.   This means
that if more gas is needed at any point, the transfer can be made.

After water, gas was the first of the utilities to go underground.
The first of the many tunnels that cross beneath the waters of New
York City was made for gas mains.   You can be sure that engineers
everywhere followed the progress of this construction with the
keenest interest, so much depended on its success.   Completed in
1894, it crosses from the Ravenswood gas plant in Long Island
City to East 71st Street, Manhattan.   It is ten feet two inches in
diameter and 2,784 feet long.   It contains one twelve inch and two
thirty-six inch gas mains.

In later years the Consolidated Gas Company, which pioneered
that first tunnel, added three more.   In 1913, it cut a mile-long
tunnel through solid rock nearly two hundred and fifty feet
below the surface of the East River.   In this tunnel are laid two
seventy-two inch mains connecting the great Astoria gas plant
on Long Island to the lower Bronx district at 132nd Street.   A third
tunnel crosses the Bronx River with two forty-two inch mains and

the fourth is under the Flushing River bearing a twenty-four inch main from the Astoria plant to Flushing. In addition to these tunnels, the Consolidated has put down five river-crossing pipe lines in the manner of the water siphon mains that cross to Staten Island.

The gas distribution system is composed of two sets of mains: the transfer mains which interconnect all the holders; and the mains that make the final delivery of gas to the consumers. The mains vary in size from two inches to seventy-two inches and are made of cast iron or steel or wrought iron. They have bell joints from 4 to 6 inches deep. The joints are filled with lead or cement to prevent any leakage. The mains are placed below the frost line. Emergency valves control the flow of gas under the most congested streets.

Gas is generally sent out under a pressure of 4 to 6 inches water column, or one-fifth of a pound per square inch. In outlying districts, however, greater pressures may be required. In such districts, regulators on the consumer's premises correct the pressure downward.

But how do the gas engineers know what point or points in the farflung system need more gas at the moment? Pressure gauges called telemetric gauges are placed at strategic places along the distributing mains. These gauges transmit the tale of their pressures by electric wires to indicators situated at the holder stations and at a central control office. The central office dispatcher watches the pressures at the transfer mains and telephones the orders that maintain an equal distribution between the plant holders and the district holders. The holder station dispatchers watch their district gauges and increase or lower pressure accordingly.

In the early days of gas, there was no device that could measure the amount of gas a customer used. He was simply charged so much a light tip. Had you lived a hundred years ago and been wealthy and broad-minded enough to have had gas illumination in your home, along about ten-thirty every evening you would have heard the gas inspector rap loudly with his cane on the sidewalk. "Lights out! Lights out!" If you did not at once obey, he himself would shut the gas off. You would then have had the choice of going to bed or lighting an oil lamp or candle.

The invention of the gas meter was a boon to both the gas company and its customers. The first meters were filled with water. They were very unsatisfactory. In the winter, the water often froze. Since alcohol added to water lowers the freezing point of the water, the gas company sold its customers whiskey at four gallons for a dollar. Can you imagine having to buy whiskey for your gas?

The principle of the dry meter which we use today was invented in 1844. The meter is divided into two lungs which, unlike our lungs, do not exhale and inhale together. While the first lung or diaphragm inhales, the second exhales. Then as the second exhausts its gas breath and begins to breathe in, the first lung begins to exhale. Each time a lung has emptied its contents into your gas range it moves a cog which records its delivery of gas. That is the record the gas man reads periodically. Look at the picture of a meter and learn how to read it. It's easy.

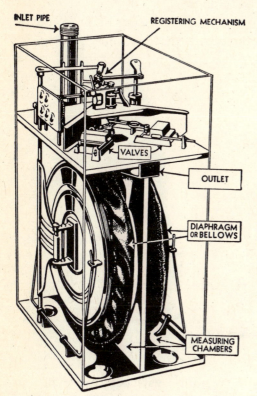

INLET PIPE  REGISTERING MECHANISM

VALVES

OUTLET

DIAPHRAGM OR BELLOWS

MEASURING CHAMBERS

### Looking Inside the Meter

This is how your meter would appear if the sides, top, front and back were removed. In the upper part is the registering mechanism; and in the lower part, the measuring chambers, consisting of two diaphragms or bellows.

The gas chemist is probably the most efficient cook in the world. You might think that cooking coal to make gas is a most wasteful process. But the coke oven gives back many useful products for every ton of coal: fifteen hundred pounds of coke;

twelve thousand cubic feet of gas; twenty-five pounds of ammonium sulphate; one and a half gallons of benzol; nine gallons of tar; and a quantity of lampblack used in the making of inks, paints and rubber. Of these by-products, the most wonderful is tar!

There used to be a time when the chemists threw the sticky, evil-smelling stuff into the rivers. Today, there are thousands of important chemicals and drugs that are drawn from it. Coal tar, properly treated, can be made into deadly explosives, delicate perfumes, poison gas, saccharin which is five hundred times as sweet as sugar, a road building material, headache remedies, carbolic acid, delightful flavoring extracts, a water-proofer, as well as dyes that rival the beautiful colors of the rainbow.

How Jean Baptiste van Helmont would stare if he could see what the modern chemist has done with that invisible "wild spirit" which he once called chaos!

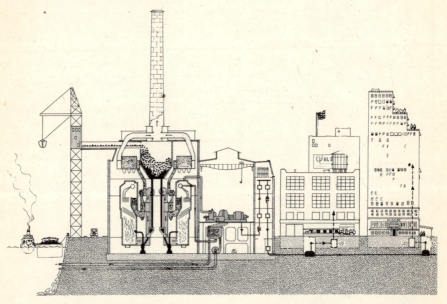

Remember, when next you turn on a gas-cock, the enormous amount of human energy, invention and research that is behind your simple action.

And above all—and always—remember:

*Turn off the gas-cock when it is not being used,*
and
*Never search for a gas leak with a flaming light.*

## Chapter 8

### City Of Wonderful Light

THE CITY IS NEVER so enchanting as at night. Darkness lays a covering hand over all that is ugly in it. Gone are the slums and the cluttered roof tops. Only the myriad lights of homes and streets remain, the spangled panels of skyscrapers, the delicately gleaming arcs spanning the black rivers, the gliding brilliance of ferry boats. Far overhead, a star, wired for sound, drones across the sky. Light! Wherever you look, shoals of light! O, City of Wonderful Light! City of Electricity! City of Power!

We know of course, that it has not always been so. If we believe that man has been an earth-being for half a million years and we let those five thousand centuries seem as one night, a night from six in the evening to six in the morning, then here is the way man lit those twelve long hours.

Until midnight or even later, he had no light at all. Then he discovered fire. A bonfire now lit his cave until about five-thirty-five A.M.

From then on, he improved his lighting rapidly, using a piece of wood flaming on one end as a kindle light, then smearing it with pitch so that it became a torch, then putting the pitch in a clay cup and lighting it as a lamp.

At this point, which might have been 600 B.C. he found that by rubbing a piece of amber, or as the Greeks called it, electron, he could use it to attract and hold pieces of cork and papyrus. This discovery was amusing but not profitable, so he went on to invent the tallow dip and the candle and the oil lamp.

At thirteen seconds before six A.M., he turned on the cock for a new lighting fuel called gas. At almost the same time, which might have been 1801, Sir Humphrey Davey invented the first electric light, an arc lamp. And just as man was thinking that this was also amusing but dangerous and impractical, along came another Englishman, young Michael Faraday, with ideas for an electricity-making machine, and then at last came our own Thomas Alva Edison with an incandescent lamp to use this electricity.

Six seconds before dawn, man pulled the cord and an electric light brilliantly dispelled the last moments of the long dark!

It seems hard to believe, but part of Fifth Avenue was lighted by gas as late as 1903.

Of course, lighting is only part of the work that electricity does, though one of the most important. Teddy Roosevelt, one time New York City Police Commissioner, said that one electric street lamp is as good as a policeman in discouraging crime. Today, we also value it as a factor in traffic safety.

Indeed, the modern metropolis would be impossible without electricity. Electric power, whether fed to subway trains, or used as a spark to explode the gasoline in an automobile or airplane engine, brings the most distant suburb within an hour's ride of the heart of the city. It provides us with highly efficient systems of communication, the telegraph, the telephone, radio, television, the moving picture. It has further shortened the horizontal spread of the city by permitting it to grow up into the air, thus giving us a new architecture and a skyline famed the world over. For skyscrapers are unthinkable without fast electric elevators.

In terms of energy, electricity provides every man, woman and child in the city with at least six invisible slaves, who work twenty-four hours a day, seven days a week, never tire, never slow up and never complain. No wonder man, who once had to work fourteen and sixteen hours a day, now works forty and even thirty-five hours a week. Engineers foresee the time when each of us will have so many of these invisible slaves that we will only have to spend two or three hours a day directing their efforts and have the rest of the day in which to enjoy a truly abundant life.

What is this Jinn, Electricity? No one knows. That is one of the mysteries about electricity. It is not a substance and yet all substances are made of it. Let's examine an atom, any atom.

Take the lightest known particle of matter, an atom of hydrogen. Don't drop it, because it is easily lost. It only weighs 0.000,-000,000,000,000,000,000,001,663 of a gram. Now give it a good smart blow. It will split into two electrical units, one of which will be 1833 times the weight of the other.

The heavier unit is a proton or positive charge of electricity. It is sluggish and prone to stick close to home. The lighter unit is an electron or negative charge of electricity. It is equal in strength with the proton. But though the two have a mania for each other's company, the electron, unlike its fat friend, leaves home readily and gaily. In fact it is the going-places of the electron that constitutes an electric current and the electron that provides the work energy of electricity.

Metals, especially copper, offer electrons the greatest freedom. In non-conductors, such as glass, paper and rubber, the electrons are tied down. The non-conductors are therefore used as insulators or fences to keep the electrons from getting through.

In any case, pluses repell each other and so do minuses. That is natural. Nobody likes to be unbalanced. Though, of course, the poles of a magnet are not plus and minus in the same sense as protons and electrons, nevertheless, they too strive continuously toward each other, with the result that the distance which keeps them apart is like a stretched rubber band. It is in tension. It has lines of force. In short, it is a magnetic field.

It was Hans Christian Oersted who discovered that electricity builds up a magnetic field about it. And it was Michael Faraday who wondered whether a magnetic field could not therefore be made to yield electricity.

For years, wherever he went, Faraday carried about with him a magnet and a piece of wire. He had tremendous faith that between the two existed the possibility of one of the world's great miracles. But how to discover it?

One day, he inserted the wire into the magnetic field between the poles of the magnet and swiftly rotated it. The lines of force were cut. The electrons on the wire, magnetically yanked about, came alive. The wire was electrically charged!

Faraday had induced an electric current out of mystery. He had done it with a moving conductor in a magnetic field. He had discovered the principle of the electric generator upon which our whole electric power age depends!

Electricity's honor roll of achievement is long and full of men of genius of every nationality. Once more, we have evidence that no one man or organized group of men can justly claim sole right to an invention or a discovery. Indeed, many people believe that inventions should belong to all humanity rather than to a few for-

tunate inventors or companies who contributed only one link in the
long chain of development.

Possibly the most commonly known name in electricity is that
of Thomas Alva Edison. It was in his laboratory that the first
practical incandescent electric lamp was made. And it was Edison
who built the first commercial electric generating plant.

It began operation on September 4, 1882, at 257 Pearl Street,
New York City. Its fifteen miles of wire were drawn through pipe
laid in shallow trenches. Four hundred street lamps and fifty-nine
customers received the first burst of juice.

Since that amazing day when people, shading their eyes against
the "blazing horseshoe" filament of the bulbs, cried out, "Won't it
explode? Don't you use any matches? Is it safe in a thunder
storm?", four thousand electric generating plants have sprung into
being in the United States. Edison's "Jumbo" sixty-kilowatt generator has grown to monstrous power, now generating one hundred
and sixty thousand kilowatts. In New York City, the fifteen miles
of wire have grown to over sixty-seven thousand miles and the
fifty-nine customers today number almost two and a half million.

Strangely enough, Edison had little to do with the growth
of his brain child. Although the Pearl Street plant could not deliver
power more than a mile away, Edison was impatient with the men
who provided the theories that gave electricity its present wide use.
His generators sent their current directly to lamps and motors.
Naturally, the current could not be sent out under high pressure
without destroying the lamps and motors. But the low pressure
limited the effective distance.

It was Charles P. Steinmetz, perhaps electricity's greatest scientist and mathematician, who showed how alternating current, a
current capable of tremendous and variable pressures, could be
generated.

In 1886, William Stanley built the first alternating current
plant in America and successfully proved that electric power could
be generated at a low pressure, transformed into a high pressure,
transmitted great distances at that pressure, then reduced to the
pressure required at the point of use. Stanley always spoke of the
transformer as the "heart of the alternating current system."

Nikola Tesla now invented the induction motor which successfully used alternating current and provided industry with the most important transmitter of power in the history of mechanics. Among the scores of other men contributing their genius to the further development of electrical practice were Elihu Thomson, who designed many of the protective devices, and Oliver Schallenberger, the inventor of the induction meter to measure the use of alternating current.

The inheritor of the New York City field of the old Edison Electric Illuminating Company (note the word, Illuminating) is the Consolidated Edison Company. Its ten city generating plants supply all but the Rockaways and the Borough of Richmond. They can generate a total of two and a half million kilowatts an hour. Two of the plants, the Hudson Avenue in Brooklyn and the Hell Gate in the Bronx, are the largest in the world. Their production alone is almost sufficient to supply the average peak loads of the city. All the plants are tied in together so that power can be shunted from any one of the plants to any one of the distributing high voltage feeders.

The Consolidated also exchanges power with the Niagara Hudson Power Corporation. The Niagara Corporation supplies power to a vast industrial valley. Since the Consolidated's peak demand comes at night, the companies are in an excellent position to help each other. Naturally, the Consolidated buys the most kilowatt hours.

Let's visit one of the Consolidated plants. They are all situated beside water in order to permit easy and cheap transportation of coal and slag waste, and because water is itself a primary raw material.

The trip begins with the boiler room. The high-pressure, five-story boilers are built and operated much as are the boilers of The New York Steam Corporation. But instead of a temperature of 430° F. at a pressure of 175 pounds per square inch, the electric plant boilers generate steam at 900° F. and a pressure of 1400 pounds. An automatic panel tells the engineer exactly how each boiler is behaving and permits him to make any necessary adjustments by simply turning a series of dials.

The steam now passes through special steel pipes to the generating floor and feeds directly into the turbines. Striking the feathered blades with the speed of a rifle bullet, it whirls them about, thus spinning the turbine shaft at exactly twenty-five, thirty, or sixty revolutions a second. A turbine turning twenty-five revolutions a second produces twenty-five cycle electricity. A turbine spinning thirty or sixty revolutions a second produces sixty cycle electricity. Because it has been determined that sixty cycle electricity is best for lighting and is more cheaply distributed, the Consolidated is gradually reducing twenty-five cycle production and will, in time, generate it only where direct current is required, as by the electrified railroads.

Since the turbine shaft is directly connected to the shaft in the adjoining generator, its mechanical energy is now converted into electrical energy.

In the direct current generator, the rotating portion is a metal core wound with many turns of wire. Fixed into the generator shell all about it are coils of wire magnetized by direct current brought in from a small direct current generator aptly called the exciter. The electrically magnetized coils set up an electric-magnetic field.

It is the lines of force of this field that the whirling armature cuts. As in Faraday's experiment, the result is electricity.

The current is drawn off by two carbon brushes each in contact with one pair of insulated slip rings, metallic rings connected to the ends of the armature wire and rotating with it. Cables attached to the brushes take the electricity out of the generator to the first step of distribution, the switching galleries.

In the alternating current generator, the rotating portion is excited by direct current and so produces the magnetic lines of force that constitute the field. The stationary portion is then the armature which both cuts the lines of force and contains the conductor which draws off the alternating current thus generated.

The alternating current dynamo is so designed that the rotor spins the first half of a revolution from a North to a South Pole, and the second half from a South to a North Pole. Since like poles repell each other, there is no electrical field between the two pluses and the two minuses. Thus, though the impetus of the rotor carries it past these empty pockets, the electric wave that is created in each half cycle goes from zero to maximum intensity and down to zero again. In short, it waxes and wanes twice in each cycle creating alternating current of twenty-five or sixty cycles, depending upon how many complete revolutions the rotor makes a second.

Not all the terrific lead-melting heat of the steam was exhausted in the high pressure turbine. Two hundred pounds of steam pressure was lost at the throttle of the turbine. In the one hundredth of a second it took to shoot through the vanes of the turbine, the steam used up 400° of heat and one thousand pounds of pressure. However, it still retains 500° of heat and two hundred pounds of pressure. That is considerable power, not to be wasted. It is therefore, directed into low pressure turbines ranging in size from 9000 to 40,000 kilowatt capacity. These use up all the rest of the steam to an almost complete vacuum and the condensed water is then returned to the boilers.

The engineers not only use the distilled water over again, they even use air over again. Cool air, blown into the generators to keep them from developing waste heat, is drawn out, water-cooled and forced back again. This process avoids the additional dust that would enter with each blast of fresh air.

And now, before we follow the current any further, let's clear up a few electrical terms, so that we will know what we are about.

What is meant when a generator is said to produce 53,000 kilowatts of power? Kilo is the Greek word for one thousand. A watt is the product of an amount of electricity times the pressure under which it is made to flow. That is like saying that a bucket is being filled with water out of an inch pipe at a pound pressure. The term for the smallest unit of electricity is ampere. The smallest unit of pressure is called a volt. A watt, then, is one ampere times one volt, and has a work energy of $\frac{1}{746}$th of a h. p.

That means that a 53,000 kilowatt generator produces over 70,000 h. p. A 160,000 kilowatt generator, the largest in use in New York City, produces over 200,000 h. p.

Since in a 53,000 kilowatt generator, the pressure or voltage may be close to 14,000 volts, the amperage or amount being manufactured, is, then, 3,785 amperes. The amount of kilowatts generated in an hour would be 53,000 kilowatt hours. By the same token a sixty watt lamp burning for an hour will consume sixty watt hours of electricity. It might be fun to see how much electric energy your home uses of an evening.

And now let's pick up the trail of the current. The current from all the generators is fed by cable through the switching galleries above the generating floor to a conductor called a bus bar. At the Hell Gate station, the bus bar, made of pure leaf copper six inches by eight inches, is six hundred feet long. It is, in effect, a collecting reservoir. All distributing mains lead from it. If it should break down, the plant would be forced out of action for there is no use pumping electricity or water into a crumbled reservoir.

Because of the tremendous importance of the bus bar, it is divided into six sections. Each section is enclosed in a fire proof concrete vault with heavy steel doors. The purpose is to confine trouble, if possible, to one section only and to safeguard the other sections in the task of distribution.

The job of the switching galleries is to switch the current from the generating cables to any section of the bus bar and to switch the current from the bus bar into designated transmission cables that take it out into the streets. The switches open and close in oil under pressure. Otherwise every operation would be accompanied by an electric arc powerful enough to destroy the system.

Before the current enters the bus, small transformers tap a tiny proportion of it and meter it. Upon leaving the bus, the current is once more proportionately metered. Thus the engineers know at all times how much they are producing and what part of it is going where. Feeder cables now take the current to the large transformers where it is stepped up to pressures as high as 132,000 volts— and at last the electricity takes to the streets. Some of the feeder cables go directly to the street.

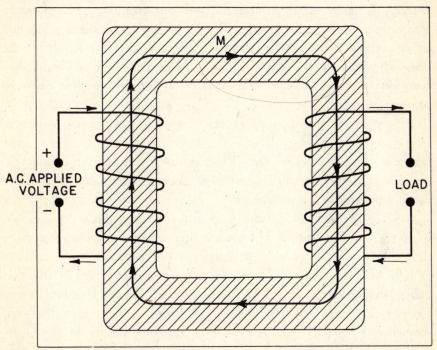

Let's have a look at the transformer. Why did Stanley call it, "the heart of the alternating system"? The answer is that it permits the current to go out under great pressure, thus carrying over a great distance, and then permits it to be divided up into pressures suitable for use. How does it do this?

Fairly simply. The transformer consists of an iron core insulated from two coils which are wound about it and insulated from each other. The coil into which the current enters is called the primary coil; the coil from which it goes on, is called the secondary coil. Induction causes the current to leap the space between the coils. When the number of turns in the secondary coil is double the number in the primary, the lines of force are doubled and so is the voltage. If, in the next transformer, the primary turns are double the secondary turns, the lines of force will be halved and the voltage will return to what it was before it entered the first transformer.

The transformer is often likened to a long shallow tank of water. Let us suppose that the bottom of a five-inch deep, twenty-foot-long tank can be opened. You put on your bathing trunks and you stand under it. The bottom is released. Down comes the water, all of it, splash! You are wet but unhurt. The pressure was only five inches  Now let's refill the tank and stand it on one of its narrow ends. You take your place under it. Ready? We open the narrow bottom. Whew! This time you are not only wet, but you are down! The water has hit you with a pressure of twenty feet.

A step-up transformer is like the tank stood upon end. A step-down transformer is like the horizontal tank with an open bottom. It will be clear, then, that in any given amount of electric current, the less pressure or voltage the more amperage, and the more voltage the less amperage.

Since in the transportation of current, long distances create a high degree of resistance and since resistance and amperage produce heat and thus waste current, it is cheaper to transmit a low amperage at high voltage. This accounts for the 132,000 voltage in the two cables that interconnect the systems of the Niagara Hudson Power Corporation and the Consolidated Edison. The conductors are carried overhead by steel towers from outside Albany to the Dunwoodie Station in Westchester. At this point, they tie in to underground oil filled cables that bring the current $11\frac{1}{2}$ miles into the terminal transformers at Hell Gate. Engineers say that not 1% of current is lost in this 150 miles of transmission. It is a good instance of the less, the more!

Let us return to the step-up transformers at the generating station. The high voltage current leaves them along underground cables or overhead wires for the sub-stations of the district. These sub-stations contain step-down transformers that bring the current down to what may be 4,000 volts or more and distribute it among feeder cables.

These cables, in turn, feed into smaller transformers that step down the voltage to 208 and send it into the grid network of cables that connects to your meter and to mine. The networks cover small districts and are independent of each other, so that trouble in one cannot interfere with service in any other. Each network may be fed from any one of several high tension feeders, thus safeguarding its supply. Networks to skyscrapers are, of course, set on end. It is as if the networks on several streets were tilted from the horizontal to the vertical.

Subways and trolleys are operated on direct current. There is also a certain amount of direct current required for special equipment in factories. For their use, alternating current is sent through a converter sub-station which takes the swing motion out of it and sends it on in an unbroken wave. Some direct current substations are equipped with standby batteries to be used in case of an emergency loss of power.

The Consolidated prefers to distribute its power by a three-phase, four-wire system. This means that the cables consist of 4 conductors. Three of these carry the live current; the fourth conductor is grounded and is neutral. This arrangement gives the Company three ways of tying in the consumer to the power mains.

If he wishes to use power for lighting only, the Company ties him in to one live conductor and the neutral. This provides him with 120 volts. If he is running machinery and so needs more power, he can get 208 volts by tapping the three live conductors, and obtain his lighting needs at the lower voltage by connecting to one live wire and the neutral.

Underground conductors are bound together in lead-sheathed cables and are insulated from each other by oil impregnated paper or rubber. Oil insures proper insulation. It is perfect for keeping out moisture and air. The high tension cables have pressure pockets of oil at every joint. The conductors of the 132,000 volt cable, each carried in a separate lead sheath, are hollow copper tubes, filled with oil at a pressure of twenty pounds.

If you are wondering how electricity can be sent through a hollow tube, the answer, I am afraid, will be most mystifying. The electrons do not travel through a conductor. They are in too much of a hurry. They shoot from atom to atom near the outside surface of the conductor! Actually, they constitute a field around the conductor. The conductor seems merely to hold them in a directed path.

Underground cables are laid in concrete banks of ducts, from four to twelve ducts to a bank. The underground transformers are also housed in heavy concrete shells.

Five submarine cables under the Harlem and East Rivers tie in Manhattan to Brooklyn, Manhattan to the Bronx, the Bronx to Queens. Tunnels carry cables from Manhattan to Queens. Two of the submarine cables are oil filled, single conductor like the Niagara power cables, and carry 27,000 volts.

All through, from the generator to your meter, the distributing system is guarded against every conceivable accident: sudden surges of power, static electricity in the air, lightning with its hammer blow of millions of volts.

Static condensers, lightning arrestors, circuit breakers, suppressors and a host of other automatic devices step into every emergency. Where they cannot wholly protect, they cut damage to a minimum.

Could you hold the reins on three and a half million horses? That is what the system operator has to do. He has three shifts of six assistants each. The nerves and controls of the entire system of the Consolidated Edison are assembled on a huge semi-circular board in a room of the Waterside Station at East River and 30th Street. This pilot board, with its motors and dials and hundreds of red and green lights, permits the operators to see just what the demand is at any one point, how it is being met, and how the equipment is behaving.

The board is divided into two parts. The upper part meters the electricity being produced in every one of the system's sixty-two generators, the amount being taken from or sent to the Niagara Hudson System, and the current flowing through the giant cables that tie the generating stations together and supply power to the railroads and the subway systems. Red and green lights indicate the positions of switches in the switching galleries and on the high voltage transmission lines which lead from the buses. The lower part of the board tells the story of the seventy-four sub-stations of the system's eighty-eight which are tied into the board.

Watching the board, the operators can tell from moment to moment what ought to be done and how to dispose their equipment. By direct telephone communication, they can open or close switches in any part of the system; they can re-route current around men making repairs or around damaged cables; they can order fires started under cold boilers; they can start more generators humming or order generators stilled. Because storm clouds bring darkness, they keep tabs on approaching storms one hundred miles away by means of long distance telephone and with the aid of a machine using radio static. There are two hours between cold boiler and spinning turbine shaft. Power must be ready the instant it is needed.

It is the task of the system operators to see that it is ready.

One of the busiest municipal offices is the Bureau of Gas and Electricity in the Department of Water Supply, Gas and Electricity. The Bureau has sole jurisdiction over the issuance of permits for all gas, steam and electrical construction overhead and underground in the City streets. Its inspectors must pass on all electrical work and installations in new buildings, as well as recheck old installations in old buildings. It examines applicants for Master Electrician's licenses and for electrician's licenses to determine their fitness. It examines and issues licenses where justified to moving picture operators. Thus the Bureau acts as our guardian against the fire hazard of defective electrical work and installation.

The Bureau is also responsible for the system of street and park lighting covering over four thousand miles of streets and some seven thousand five hundred acres of parks. The lights go on and off automatically according to a schedule fixed by the Bureau. They are serviced by contractors.

One of the most important vigils which the Bureau keeps is against electrolysis. Electrolysis is a condition caused by stray electric currents which jump from defective connections of the third rail in the underground railroads to nearby water mains. This deteriorates the mains. By timely detection of electrolysis conditions, the Bureau is able to safeguard our water system of four thousand five hundred miles of mains against breakdown with its expense and possible injury to life and property.

The special importance of electric power is that its energy can be transmitted great distances and that it is the cheapest of all known motor forces. That is why it has taken such rapid possession of the earth. Remotest countries are beginning to employ their water power to produce electricity.

Sixty to seventy percent of the electric current in the United States is still produced by steam turbine. And yet we have enough water power to generate one hundred and fifty billion kilowatt hours per year. At present we are only getting one third of that power, but our government has built and is still building huge dams to provide us with more and cheaper electricity. For cheap electricity is one of the surest paths to a richer standard of living.

# PART IV

# PUBLIC COMMUNICATIONS

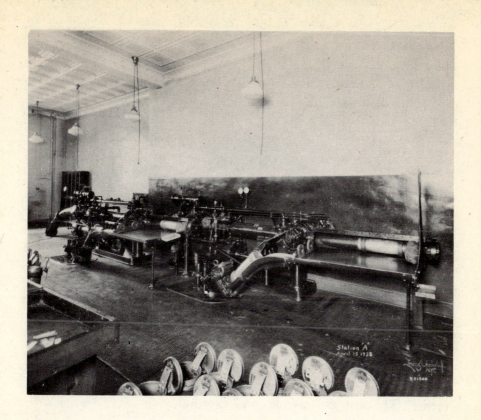

Chapter 9

Chute The Mail!

*"Neither snow nor rain nor heat nor gloom of night stays these couriers from the swift completion of their appointed rounds."*

You will find this noble sentence carved into the marble of the General Post Office of New York City. It was written by Herodotus, the wise reporter of the ancient world, some two thousand four hundred years ago in admiration of the messengers of a great Persian king.

How aptly it describes the resolution of all couriers before and since!

Yet the runners of King Sargon, five thousand years ago, were sometimes delayed, if not halted, by the forces of nature. More often, they had to contend with ferocious bandits or treasonable men anxious to learn the King's intention. If they lost, the message never arrived.

The riders of the pony express carrying the commands of Ghenghis Khan across the entire continent of Asia, across Russia to the conquering horde in Hungary, even these fierce, tireless men sometimes fell by the wayside, victims of the elements, of accidents, of treachery.

More than six hundred years later, our own Pony Express riders still faced the same enemies: weather, chance and man. So did the high leather-hung stagecoach. So did the Iron Horse.

Not until fifty years ago did the boast of the mail carriers become a fact; and then only within the confines of a city. Between communities, the mail still faces the hazards of flood, snow, storm, fog and human frailty.

But how can these dangers be avoided even within a city? Surely, the weather is always with us. Where can one escape the storm? The answer is simple: underground.

Birney Clark Batcheller is the engineer who designed the first underground pneumatic mail tube in America. It was a six-inch tube installed in 1893 in Philadelphia between the General Post Office and a branch post office half a mile away at 6th and Chestnut Streets. Having proved its worth, Batcheller then designed an eight-inch tube for New York City. The first extension was put into operation in 1897 between the General Post Office and the Produce Exchange. There followed an extension to Grand Central Station and another to the General Post Office in Brooklyn. The tube to Brooklyn was carried across the East River over the Brooklyn Bridge. In a few years, the pneumatic mail tube system extended as it now does from the Battery to 125th Street.

Most of the post offices have a receiving tube and a sending tube connecting to the post office just before and another pair of receiving and sending tubes to the post office just ahead.

The tubes are made of heavy cast iron pipe, bored to a very smooth inside surface of eight and one-eighth inches. They are laid side by side on wooden blocks in a trench below the frost line.

Bends have an inside surface of eight and three-eighths inches and a radius of eight feet, a curve wide enough not to slow the carrier. They are protected by brick or concrete housing. Their bell joints are caulked with lead. This makes them sufficiently flexible and proof against the tremors that occasionally pass through the City's base.

The mail carriers are steel cylinders twenty-four inches long with an inside diameter of seven inches. They are driven through the tube by an air pressure of 4 to 8 pounds per square inch. This pressure is provided by electrically driven air compressors and rotary blowers in eleven power stations spaced over the fifty-four mile route of twenty-three post offices.

Each of these post offices is equipped with a receiving and sending apparatus. To be sent, a carrier is placed in the sending scoop of the transmitter. This scoop is set at a steep angle in the floor. The buffer end of the carrier rests against a closed gate. This gate opens automatically at intervals of eleven and a half seconds, thus avoiding collisions. As it opens, the carrier drops into an air chamber. Air pressure then drives it through a lower gate and into the tube where the swift current of air carries it to the next station. The current of air may be likened to the current of a river, except that it is much faster.

The air shoots the mail through the core of the City at between thirty and forty miles an hour.

That is quite some speed! What brakes it at the receiving end? There are two types of receivers, the open and the closed receiver. In the open receiver, the carrier is brought to rest by the friction created in its swing around an open, circular trough made of a half section of tube.

In the closed receiver, the carrier, rushing toward the dead end gate of the tube, piles up an air cushion ahead of it. This air cushion brakes it and at the same time forces the gate open. The carrier pops through at the reduced rate of one mile per hour.

The tubes were built and are still owned by the New York Mail and Newspaper Transportation Company. Up to 1939, this Company not only leased the tubes to the Government, but also operated them. Since then, it's employees have become Government employees and the Company merely maintains the tubes.

They are operated week days between five A.M. and ten P.M. and carry about 6 to 7 million letters a day. Of course, their service was much more important in the days of the horse-drawn mail wagon. Today, when streets are kept open in the severest snow storms and mail trucks can make bulk delivery in almost the same time as the tubes, their usefulness is not quite so great. Indeed, the U.S. Post Office has stopped using pneumatic tubes in all cities save New York City and Boston.

And yet, pneumatic tubes retain some advantages over truck delivery. Whereas a truck will dump a load of letters on the sorting tables, rushing the sorters and yet making them wait between truck loads, the chute provides a steady flow of mail. Another thing, on short hauls, as between the main post office and Grand Central, a carrier will whisk mail to the trains in five minutes where a truck might take half an hour to buck the street traffic between these points.

Something of the same loss in importance has been suffered by the 28 miles of tubes used by the Western Union Telegraph Company. Indeed, some of the branch offices formerly on the tube line have been disconnected. The teleprinter, which electrically records messages typed at some distance from it, is both faster and cheaper in operation.

The Western Union owns and operates pneumatic tubes in many cities. These tubes are of copper or of seamless steel, two and a quarter inches in diameter, and are laid in creosoted wood ducts. The carrier is made of a fiber tubing, eight inches long and one and five-eighth inches in diameter. It enters the tube at intervals of two seconds. Air pressure gives it a speed of 20 to 40 miles an hour.

The telegraph tubes are blocked more often than the mail

tubes. The reason is that messenger boys sometimes drop chewing gum, rubber bands and erasers into the inlets. If a carrier jams, pressure is doubled and sometimes reversed. If that doesn't dislodge it, a heavy carrier may be shot against it, or it may have to be poked out with a steel rod. In any case, this bit of fun costs money and time and the Company does its best to discourage it.

Western Union was the first to build a pneumatic tube in New York City. That was in 1876, twenty-three years after London had installed a telegraph pneumatic tube line. However, the honors for the invention of pneumatic transmission belong to Denis Papin who described the method in 1667 in a paper presented before the Royal Society of London.

There was a time when the New York office of the Associated Press, one of the world's great news-gathering agencies, snapped its dispatches to the local newspaper offices by air chute. Even newspapers were once delivered in the carriers. But every invention has to justify its usefulness from day to day. The pneumatic tube has been an important factor in speeding the written word. It still is important, but not nearly as much so. New inventions, cheaper in operation, faster, may in time drive it into the limbo of forgotten things.

Meanwhile, how exciting to remember that, as we walk the streets, millions of letters and thousands of written telegrams, many bearing the stamp of fate, are shooting every which way under our very feet! The streets of a city are alive in more ways than people usually imagine.

## Chapter 10

### Don't Write, Telegraph!

"I'LL PUT A GIRDLE ROUND about the world in forty minutes!"

That is Puck's brag in "A Midsummer Night's Dream." And splendid for *you*, Puck! In Shakespeare's day the most rapid method to girdle little England with the joyous news of the destruction of Spain's Invincible Armada was to use fire beacons lit on hill after hill. And good enough, Puck, two hundred and fifty years later when cannon, stationed all along the Mohawk trail and down the Hudson River, blasted the glad news to New Yorkers that the Erie Canal had been opened at Buffalo. That message took twice your forty minutes to traverse the three hundred and fifty miles.

But today, Puck, your boast is a confession of old age. Today, using an electric impulse, we can girdle the world in one-seventh of a second. By telegraph or telephone wire or by radio we can flash around the world 16,800 times while you are plodding your way around it once.

It was no accident that the invention of the electric telegraph came at the beginning of the Power Age, when distances were being telescoped by unheard of speeds. Railroads were fast replacing stagecoaches. Steamships were beginning to be taken more seriously by sailing men. The time was ripe for the speeding up of communications. Letters, even when carried by steam engines, had become too slow.

The word telegraph is a blend of two Greek words, *tele,* which means "far off," and *grapho,* which means "to write." Telegraphy then, is the art of recording a message afar. The beacons of England and the cannons booming down the Hudson were telegraphy. What the world was waiting for, however, was electric telegraphy.

Charles Morrison, a Scottish surgeon, was probably the first to outline a plan for an electric telegraph. That was in 1753, too early in the history of electricity. The first long distance telegraph line was constructed forty-three years later by a Spaniard, Don Francisco Salva. But still not enough was known about electricity. French, German, English and American inventors tried to solve the problem.

No real progress was made, however, until the Swedish scientist, Hans Christian Oersted, discovered that electricity can magnetize iron. And now, William Sturgen of England was able to make an electromagnet by winding a piece of copper wire around a bar of iron. Electricity shot into the coil of wire magnetized the bar.

Joseph Henry of Albany, New York, took this invention a step further by increasing the number of coils and so making an electromagnet that could operate at a distance. The telegraph as we know it was now definitely taking shape. For that is all that the old-fashioned telegraph was, an electromagnet operated from afar.

The most promising work in the next few years was done by the physicist, Sir Charles Wheatstone and by Professor Samuel Finley Breese Morse, a well-known American artist, some of whose paintings you can see at the Metropolitan Museum of Art in New

York City. Of the two telegraph systems, the Morse was destined to prove best.

The idea for it first came to the artist in 1832 while he was tossing on the Atlantic. Some years later, he was joined by the young inventor, Alfred Vail, and together, pooling their industry and imagination, they set to work perfecting the electric telegraph. In 1838, Morse demonstrated it to the President of the United States, Van Buren, and his cabinet, and requested Congressional support. Our Representatives took five years to consider the merits of the project and then granted thirty thousand dollars to pay for the stringing of the first commercial telegraph line in America.

On May 24, 1844, Vail awaited at the Baltimore end of the wire the first message from his friend and partner in Washington, D.C. While the members of Congress looked on, Morse, reflecting his humble estimate of his own part in the wonderful invention, tapped out the message: "What God hath wrought!"

You may be sure that the Congressmen were deeply impressed by the event. But when Morse offered to sell his invention to the Government for one hundred thousand dollars it was their opinion that the device could not be made to pay for itself.

Businessmen, however, were quick to see its value. They could now keep in close touch with all markets and buy and sell with telegraphic speed. Reporters welcomed it. Their stories could now travel from event to press at the rate of 186,000 miles a second. Government departments gladly availed themselves of this instant method of communication in a rapidly expanding country. So eager were the railroads to employ the telegraphic nerve, that they gladly provided the telegraph companies with free right of way along their tracks in exchange for telegraph communications necessary to run their trains and carry on their business.

Congress had rejected Government ownership of a public utility that was some day to be of more vital importance than the service of the United States Post Office.

By 1851 there were fifty telegraph companies in the United States, most of them using the Morse patents.

The Western Union Telegraph Company came into being in 1851. By 1856, it had absorbed thirteen companies operating in the Midwest; and upon obtaining the right to install the simpler Morse instrument, it proceeded to build a national network.

The march of its eight million telegraph poles reached the Pacific Ocean at the outbreak of the Civil War, thus uniting East and West at the very moment when North and South divided. The first message carried by the new line was from the Chief Justice of California to Abraham Lincoln in Washington, promising that California would fight for the Union. A grand beginning for a national telegraph!

Incidentally, the Pony Express riders, who had heretofore galloped telegrams and other important communications from St. Joseph to San Francisco, lost their jobs to the galvanized iron wire swinging over prairies, deserts and mountains. So glorious is their page in the history of pioneer days that it is hard to believe that Buffalo Bill and his companions wrote it all in a brief eighteen months.

Gradually, Western Union bought out all of its rivals. Today its land wires and ocean cables form the greatest telegraph system in the world.

Suppose we have a peek at the past. It is in the days before

the telephone. Your great-grandfather, pulling at his young side-
burns, stands before a small telegraph call-box attached to a wall
in the hall of his home. He is wondering whether he dare send a
birthday telegram to a girl in Yorkville.

Finally he decides to do so. The call-box has a circular face
with numbered dials. Its wires lead to the offices of the American
District Telegraph Company. Your G.G.F. does not twist dial
number one, for that would cause the A.D.T. to send the fire engines
to his home. He does not bother with dial number two, for then the
A.D.T. would send the police. Instead he turns dial number three.

Soon an A.D.T. boy appears. The Western Union had no
messenger boys of its own until some time in the '90's. The boy
carries the telegram to the nearest Western Union office.

There the Morse operator begins sending the telegram to the
Yorkville office. His transmitter is simply a device that closes and
opens an electric circuit. When he presses the sending key down,
the circuit is closed and current flows along the connecting wire
to the receiving instrument in Yorkville. There the electric current
magnetizes a soft iron bar which attracts a tiny hammer that strikes
against a bracket with a click.

When the operator lifts his finger from the sending key, a
spring pulls it up, thus breaking the circuit, stopping the current,
demagnetizing the iron bar and releasing the hammer. That completes the Morse dot. When the operator holds the key down a
moment longer, that is the dash. It is these dots and dashes that
make up the Morse code.

There was a time when the clicking hammer had a pen attached
to it. The pen marked the dots and dashes on a strip of moving
paper. Then a very fast sending key was invented which telegra-
phists came to call a "bug" because it could be made to buzz the
click as continuously as an insect buzzes. Vail followed that by
contriving the sounder box, insisting that operators could be taught
to listen to the buzz and that telegraphy would thus be greatly
speeded. He proved to be right.

That is why the Yorkville operator is able to receive your
G.G.F.'s message without so much as glancing at the telegraph instrument. An A.D.T. boy now rushes it to its final destination.

A pretty girl in flounces and bustle accepts it happily.   She writes a reply.

TO: GGF

MANY THANKS COULD YOU SAY THESE NICE THINGS AT DINNER TONIGHT

GGM

When the impatient man reads this telegram, he rushes to the call-box and dials number four.   In due time, A.D.T. sends a public hack around.   G.G.F. leaps into it.   "Don't spare the horse!" he cries.   Perhaps that evening he proposes to the girl you now think of as great-grandma.

The telegraph has been through many changes since that day. The A.D.T. no longer tries to be all things to all men.   Today, it confines itself to such matters as installing and servicing telegraphic fire alarms and burglar alarm systems in buildings.   The telegraph company has its own messenger corps.   The great forests of cedar and chestnut poles that once carried the telegraph wires through our streets are almost forgotten.   Telegraph lines are now, with few exceptions, underground.

The most extraordinary changes, however, have taken place in the field of sending and receiving instruments.   Automatic printing telegraph devices have largely replaced the bug and sounder. The wire that once carried a single message at a time, then two, then four by grace of Edison's ingenuity, now carries eight and even one hundred and forty-four at a time!   "Faster!   And cheaper!" has been the cry of the twentieth century, and the telegraph engineer has responded by creating one miracle after another.

The simplest way to see how the modern telegraph operates is to watch a telegram from sender to receiver.   But before we do that let's see how the telegraph offices are tied together.

Most telegraph circuits need only one wire, the return being made through the earth by grounding the far end.   Water mains make fine grounds and so are most often used to complete the circuits.   Telegraph wires entering an office are grouped on a switchboard to which are also attached the wires leading to the telegraph instruments in the office.   The connections between these sets of wires, however, are made on a distributing rack just behind the switchboard. Because there is danger that lightning or a stray earth current may enter the office through the incoming wire and possibly do damage to the office equipment, each incoming wire is provided with an arrester and a fuse before it reaches the switchboard. The arrester drains all excess voltages into the earth.

The amount of electricity that animates a telegraph wire is astonishingly small. The automatic devices operate on a direct current of one-eighteenth of an ampere at 160 volts, or less than nine watts of power. That power, however, must never fail. The telegraph company is therefore prepared to meet any failure on the part of the electric power cables entering its plant. Emergency power is assured by storage batteries capable of providing sufficient electricity to operate the equipment and light the work for 48 hours. Beyond that, gasoline-engine-driven electric generators can take up the load.

In the days when wires were strung like fantastic warps above our city streets, telegraph service was often interrupted by storms. If you will step into the Museum of the City of New York, you will see a very realistic model of the financial district during the famous blizzard of 1888. Telegraph and telephone poles have been knocked about like toothpicks and the snarled and broken wires lie useless in the snow. That blizzard caused the companies to accept Edison's suggestion that all wires in the city be put underground. They had in any case been wondering how they could possibly add more wires to the overcrowded air above the streets.

Today, telegraph wires, carefully wrapped in paper and cotton insulation, and packed up to 455 pairs of wires to a lead-sheathed, moistureproof cable, are laid snugly four or more feet below the surface of the street.

Cables are manufactured to reach exactly from one manhole to the next. Between manholes, which are about a block apart, the cables run through ducts of vitrified clay or creosoted wood, concreted over for utmost protection.

Manholes may be just big enough for one man to work in or may be the size of a large room. In any case the cable worker faces a most taxing job. In splicing or connecting the ends of the cables he has to be sure that the wire going to Allentown, Pennsylvania, keeps going there and does not get itself attached to a wire bound for New Orleans or to any one of hundreds of other wires.

Every wire splice he makes has to be insulated. When the joints have all been made, he pours hot parrafin over them to boil out all moisture and air, wraps them in muslin, covers the whole with a lead sleeve, and finally solders the sleeve to the lead sheath. By gently rubbing or "wiping" the hot lead joints, often for as long as half an hour, he makes certain that no pores remain in them through which air or moisture can enter the cable.

In later years, he will test the cable for leaks by forcing a harmless gas into it. If the gas escapes he will find the faulty point and repair it. His motto is: A sealed cable always and forever!

And now let's send a few telegrams and see how they are handled. There are several ways of getting a telegram to a telegraph office. If you have a telephone at home, you can call Western Union and dictate your message. You can also call from a coin box telephone.

In either case you will enter the main telegraph office through a marvellous little switchboard which will automatically connect you to an operator who is unoccupied. She will type your message on a noiseless machine, read it back to you, tell you what it costs, then place it on a telegraph conveyer and start it off to the location in the building where an operator will transmit it toward its destination.

You may, of course, step into a branch office and actually see your telegram get under way. If the office is below 14th St., your message may be dropped into a pneumatic tube under the counter, shoot under the city streets and be received at the main office half a minute later. If the branch office is above 14th Street, and is not connected by tube to the main office, your telegram will be given to an operator to type out on a machine that looks like a typewriter. This is the teleprinter. As fast as your message is typed, it goes out over a telegraph wire to the main office where a receiving machine automatically types it on a yellow blank.

If the message is to be relayed to a branch office on the pneumatic tube line, it is thrust into a small container, and dropped into the chute going to the branch office. If it is addressed to a city office having no tube connection, it will be immediately sent out on the teleprinter connected to that office.

If you are in a business office, you may have three ways of getting a telegram to the telegraph office. You can telephone. You can use the Western Union callbox. Or you can send your message by teleprinter. You already know how the telephone call will be handled. When you turn the handle of the call box, your identification number is automatically written on a tape in the company's nearest branch office. A card file tells the office manager who is calling, whereupon he sends a boy to get your telegram.

Many businesses, particularly the press, which does a great deal of news gathering by telegraph, are tied into the telegraph office by one or more teleprinters. This enables them to send and receive telegrams in the fastest possible time.

Whichever path your telegram takes, we will assume that it has arrived at the pneumatic tube terminal in the main office. Let's look in at the terminal room in Western Union's handsome brick building at 60 Hudson Street. If your telegram is to a friend in the city living near a branch office on the tube line, the carrier bearing it is rerouted to that office. Otherwise, it is extracted from the container by men wearing gloves and using pincers and started on its way to the sorting belts.

This belt system carries fourteen vertical divisions into which young women rapidly sort the telegrams according to their destinations. Off they go to the particular department that will speed them on their way. Each department re-sorts its batch of telegrams. Then girls, on noiseless, easy-moving roller skates, distribute them among the telegraph operators, giving each operator only those messages which can be sent over her wires. Each operator has a small switchboard which enables her to connect her sending or receiving instrument with any one of the local offices assigned to her.

If your telegram is to a friend in a small community where the only telegraph office is at the railroad station, it may be sent by Morse telegraph. Up to 1910, over ninety percent of Western Union's messages were tapped out on the "bug," but today fewer than five percent reach a sounder. A glance at the few operators in the Morse division at 60 Hudson Street will tell you most convincingly that Morse telegraphy has no future. There are no young people among them. The young people are at the slick, lacquered automatic machines.

Your telegram, if it is addressed to an office where traffic is heavy, will go to one of these young women operating a multiplex telegraph machine. This machine is one of four sending and four receiving machines all on one wire and connected to four receiving and four sending machines at the other end of the wire. Thus eight messages can be sent at the same instant over the one wire. But how is that possible? How are the messages kept from jumbling like half a dozen jig-saw puzzles in a gale?

Let's follow the telegrams being sent by operators A, B, C, D, in New York City to operators A, B, C, D, in San Francisco. As each operator strikes the keys of her typewriter-like machine, a code number of holes representing each letter is punched into a narrow, moving paper strip. The strip enters the multiplex transmitter, where electric contacts form at every hole. Instantly, electric impulses flash out over the wire to the receiver at San Francisco.

There these impulses are translated into ordinary print automatically typed on a moving tape.

The distribution of correct letters from sender A to receiver A, and from B to B, and so on, is made by two wheels each at the opposite ends of the wire. These wheels, revolving at high speed, establish one circuit at a time, break it and pass on to the next. Each revolution of the wheels, therefore, makes and breaks four circuits. Thus the four messages are sent and received together, one letter or space at a time each in succession.

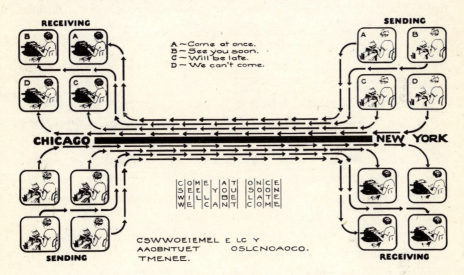

At the same time, four operators in San Francisco may be sending messages to 60 Hudson Street on the same wire because "differential relays" prevent receiving instruments at each station from responding to signals from the transmitters at the station. Up to six hundred words a minute going in two directions between sixteen machines may pass over the one wire.

As rapidly as your telegram appears on the receiving tape, the tape is gummed on a yellow blank. In a few moments it is on the way to your friend.

Since an electric current grows feebler with distance, all long distance circuits have repeater stations to boost the current. The stations are 200 to 300 miles apart. While crossing the continent your telegram may be revived at Harrisburg and Pittsbugh, Pa.; Columbus, Ohio; Indianapolis and Vincennes, Indiana; St. Louis and Kansas City, Mo.; Ellis, Kansas; Denver and Grand Junction, Colo.; Salt Lake City, Utah; Elko and Reno, Nevada; and San Francisco. It is like the Pony Express rider changing his exhausted horse for a fresh animal while the contents of his mail bag remain the same.

Compare the thirty words a minute that a fast Morse operator can send along one wire with the six hundred of the Multiplex system. Telegraph lines are expensive to build and maintain. That is why the engineers have always striven to make each wire carry as much traffic as possible. Edison, one of telegraphy's wizards, holder of thirteen hundred patents in this one field, once invented a way to send 3,100 words a minute. But even that has been eclipsed by the modern carrier system which can accommodate 6,600 words a minute on one wire!

No wonder rates are so much lower than they were directly after the Civil War. Then, a ten-word telegram between San Francisco and New York City cost $7.45; today, the rate is $1.20.

You know, of course, that sound travels in vibrating waves and that the difference between one pitch and another is the difference between the number of their vibrations a second. Telegraph engineers have found that messages sent on pitches three hundred vibrations apart will not interfere with each other. Each pitch can be tuned in at the receiving end of the wire just as you tune your wireless radio to the kilocycles of a particular radio station.

This very simple discovery has provided them with thirty-six channels on a pair of wires. And since each channel can serve to connect four sending and four receiving machines of the multiplex system, it is now possible to send 288 messages at one time over the same pair of wires. Messages on a carrier wire flow in both directions.

Nevertheless, the system of tens of thousands of miles of wire now interconnecting our cities is eventually slated to go. It will be replaced by radio beam channels operated from towers a hundred feet high and built on promontories 30 to 50 miles apart. These super high-frequency channels will not be affected by electric storms or by sun spots and will carry as large a load of messages as do wires. Soon the first triangular radio telegraphic network will be in operation between New York, Washington, D.C., and

Pittsburgh. The cross-country forest of telegraph poles will some day join the past with the buffalo and the Pony Express.

An ingenious crew, these engineers! They have developed a facsimile telegraph named the Telefax for public use. The writer of the telegram need only press a button on the machine and drop the telegram into a slot which has opened to receive it. The message is automatically wrapped around a cylinder. A tiny photographic eye moves lengthwise across the revolving cylinder, registering all dark and light on a chemically treated blank at the main office. The process takes about two minutes.

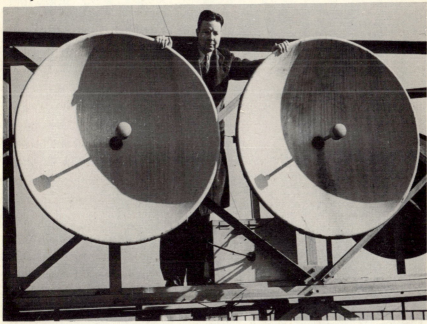

Western Union also has a nation-wide system of electrically synchronized clocks which take their time from local master clocks corrected from signals by the United States Naval Observatory in Washington, D.C. In a shock proof vault deep under 60 Hudson Street are two pendulum clocks each six feet in diameter. These huge master clocks are regulated to tick off every sixtieth of a second in perfect unison with the clock at the Naval Observatory. If anything were to happen to the Observatory clock, the nation's radio stations, railroads, air fields, business houses and research laboratories would be able to get the correct time during the emergency from the Western Union clocks. These Western Union clocks are situated in every important city in the country. The city master clocks, in turn, regulate the accuracy of the many clocks to which they are electrically connected.

One of the oldest and most important telegraph services is performed by the Western Union stock tickers. I am not here referring to our custom of crowning parading heroes with spirals of ticker tape. The ticker has a more serious purpose in life. Improved by Edison at the very beginning of his career, it supplies its user with instant news of transactions in the stock exchanges and the commodity markets of the country.

This central copper wire carries the electric current. If it breaks, these flexible copper tapes carry the current around the gap.

This is the permalloy tape whose wonderful magnetic qualities keep the signals from jumbling. A thick covering of gutta-percha holds the currents to their path.

A wrapping of jute cushions the pressure of three miles of sea-water.

Eighteen steel armor-wires protect the cable from injury.

Last of all a wrapping of tarred hemp cords, then the soft ooze of the ocean's floor.

Today it is a vastly improved machine in a system that ties three hundred and fifty cities and towns into a national network. It has a speed of five hundred characters a minute, more than sufficient to report the transactions even of the biggest markets. So vital is the ticker service to the business man of the country that a duplicate transmitting plant, having its own power, is always ready to pinch hit in any emergency.

No other portion of telegraphic history is quite so exciting, so full of adventure, suspense and bitter disappointment, and so grand in its final accomplishment, as the story of the transoceanic cables. It was our friend Don Francisco Salva who first seriously suggested that they were possible.

In 1842, Morse tried laying a cable on the harbor floor between Governors Island and the Battery. A ship's anchor snapped it. In 1850, a cable crossing the English channel between Dover and Calais actually established communications. A fisherman caught it and cut off a section. To him it was a "speciman of rare seaweed, with its center filled with gold."

In the next few years, however, short cables were successfully put down and kept in operation between Dover and Calais, between Sweden and Denmark, and between points on the Mediterranean sea.

Now began the saga of the transatlantic cables. Three men, the American financier, Cyrus W. Field, the English engineer, Charles Bright, and the brilliant young English scientist, Professor William Thomson, staked fortune and good repute on their common dream of joining Europe and America by wire. As always, there were scientists and knowing laymen to ridicule such an undertaking and to declare it in every way mad and impossible. And so for a while it seemed.

Both the British and American navies cooperated in the first attempt to lay a cable. But after the U.S. Frigate Niagara, starting at Valentia, on the west coast of Eire, had paid out three hundred and eighty miles of the cable, it encountered an ocean valley more than two miles deep. The conductor snapped.

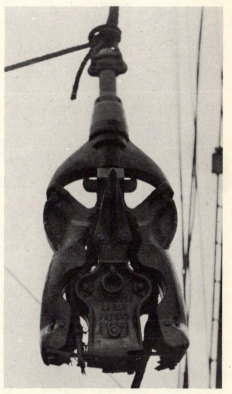

Disheartened but undeterred, Field, Bright and Thomson were back on the job in the summer of the following year, 1858. Five times they tried and five times the cable snapped or was lost on the ocean floor. The sixth try was successful. The British ship Agamemnon, which had been having all the trouble, finally landed her end of the cable at Valentia, while the Niagara anchored her end at Heart's Content, Newfoundland.

The first official transatlantic telegraph message was sent from England on August 15, 1858. "Europe and America are united by telegraphy. Glory to God in the highest, on earth peace, good will toward men."

Three months later the cable ceased to operate. The insulation had been destroyed by the 2,000 volts of current which was incorrectly thought necessary to send a message across the 1,900 miles of gray Atlantic.

Undaunted, Field and his friends examined their task more closely and reorganized their forces. At last, in 1865, and in 1866, their perseverance and vision were rewarded. They succeeded in laying not one, but two cables! Since they first showed the way, 3,500 cable lines, 360,000 miles long, have spanned the waters of the world. Man's word courses the deeps of all the oceans of the earth faster than a dolphin's leap!

Many of the twenty-one transatlantic cables, after coming up at Newfoundland, dive into the sea again and do not come up until they reach New York City waters. Not until 1924 was any important change made in their construction. In that year, Western Union laid a cable from New York to the Azores that had a wafer-thin ribbon of an alloy of iron and nickel, called permalloy, wound about the copper conductor. This magnetic coil increased the sending speed from three hundred letters a minute to fifteen hundred.

In 1926, a new cable of the same design shot the letter speed up to twenty-four hundred. In 1928, by ending the permalloy short of the ends of a new cable to the Azores, the Western Union brought the speed up to fourteen hundred letters each way. As in land cables, repeaters are used at all land points to revive the strength of messages. The vastly increased speed as well as the constant traffic has reduced London to New York rates from the one hundred dollar minimum in 1866 to sixty cents, the day-rate for five code words today.

There are today forty-five specially built cable ships maintaining the transoceanic cables of the world. Of these, the most remarkable is the Lord Kelvin. This ship bears the later name of William Thomson, who was made a Lord in honor of his great contribution to the arts of peace. The Lord Kelvin not only does what any good cable ship is designed to do, it does one thing more. It plows cables under the floor of the ocean!

Ever since 1890 when the new steam trawlers began dragging their heavy iron-shod trawls through the fish-live waters off Cape Clear, Eire, the many cables sweeping in from Newfoundland, Penzance, Le Havre, Brest, Calais, Emden and the Azores have often been injured. Even a tiny break is enough to fault a cable. The task of locating the break, cutting the fault out and splicing in a new section of cable, is a costly one. The cable companies have often petitioned the English government to send the trawlers elsewhere. No wonder the cablemen and the fishermen have never liked one another.

In 1934, Western Union engineers built the first sea plow man had ever seen. The Lord Kelvin's crew of ninety men began to practice with it. One morning four years later, after many changes in the design of the plow, they set to work on 4-PZ, the heaviest traffic-bearing cable in the North Atlantic. The great ten and a half ton plow, carrying the cable in its nose, dug a furrow about two feet deep along a carefully surveyed route on the ocean bottom off Valentia. As rapidly as the cable entered the opening trench, the waters rolled the soil over it where no trawl could snag it. By nightfall, the anxious cablemen had completed their assignment. They had plowed under all that part of the cable that had been faulted fourteen times in thirteen years. A new era in cable laying had begun.

It may be some time before all the cables off Cape Clear are so safeguarded that cablemen and fishermen can meet and smile. The cable landings at Newfoundland are not yet troubled by deep sea trawlers. You may be sure that if ever they are, the cable ships will plow under all cable ends. That is one way of bringing "on earth peace, good will toward men."

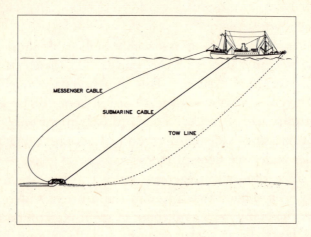

It is interesting to note that today neither Morse nor Field are represented by a single descendant in the companies that have inherited the fruits of their genius. Nevertheless, the world will do them honor long after its complex social, political and business life shall cease to flow along the thin copper conductor that they once laid on land and sea.

## Chapter 11

## Hello! The Telephone

YOU LIFT THE RECEIVER.

"Number, please?"

You give the number you are calling. If you are using a dial phone, you dial the number. In any case it is like naming the target at which you wish to aim. In thirty seconds or so, the invisible target pops up. "Hello!" it says. "Hello!" you cry, and your voice strikes it square in the very center.

If your call is within New York City, it has had to find its way through a maze of nine and a quarter million miles of copper wire. It has had to select one telephone among more than two million instruments. If your call has gone out over long distance lines to some friend in the United States, it has had to find his telephone among nearly twenty-eight million others. Yet it has done so, and you are not in the least amazed!

Indeed, if your needle in the haystack had not at once said "Hello! Here I am!" you would have been annoyed. So commonplace is the miracle of the telephone to most of us.

I know that you will agree that we take for granted too many of the marvels about us. And this is not because we are so well acquainted with them; on the contrary, it is because we know so little about them.

Let's look at the telephone. What is it? It is a mechanical mouth and ear that enables us to converse over an electric circuit with anyone else having a like mouth and ear. Behind this simple definition is the solid body of research and invention by hundreds upon hundreds of men whose labors, when added together, have given us one of the most complex instruments that man has ever devised.

As an animal, man has always been able to make sounds, but it is only in the last hundred years that he has begun to understand the nature of sound. Sound travels in waves of vibrating air. Every sound and every pitch has its own number of vibrations. As the sound enters the ear, the air waves vibrate against the delicate eardrum, causing it to vibrate in exact sympathy with them. A nerve leading to the brain translates the vibrations into sound.

Once having understood these mechanics, men in Europe and America began to think of ways to send sound over distance and to receive it. In 1854, Charles Bourseul of France wrote that "if one spoke near a moveable disc sufficiently flexible to lose none of the vibrations of the voice, this disc, by alternately making and breaking the current from a battery, might cause another disc at a distance, to execute the same vibrations simultaneously."

For twenty-one years, inventors tried to put this formula into practice. The most notable among them was the poor German schoolteacher, Philip Reis, who is honored by his nation as the true inventor of the telephone. In 1860, he demontrated an instrument in which the receiver was an artificial ear composed of a pig's ear and human ear bones. However, all he was able to hear with it was a musical pitch.

Not until Alexander Graham Bell had corrected Bourseul's formula was the telephone actually conceived. Young Bell was a

Scot living in Boston who specialized in vocal science and in teaching the deaf to speak. He recognized that a telephone current must *not* be alternately made and broken as in telegraphy. It must be unbroken. What was required was to make a "current of electricity vary in intensity as the air varies in density during the production of sound."

That was what he said to twenty-one-year-old Thomas A. Watson, the mechanic who was helping him to work out his ideas for a telegraph that could send several messages at different musical pitches along one wire. Bell called it the "Harmonic Telegraph"; but as Watson tells of it, it usually kicked up a "row as if all the miseries this world of trouble ever produced were concentrated there." Bell went stubbornly on trying to get more harmony into his contrivances. Watson continued to make change upon change in the apparatus, and the telephone idea slumbered.

Then one afternoon, while the harmonic seemed possessed of half a dozen screeching fiends, a miracle occurred. The two men were working at opposite ends of a wire connecting two rooms about sixty feet apart. Watson was at the transmitter. Bell was at the receiver. Watson was plucking at a transmitter spring to make it vibrate. Suddenly Bell shouted and rushed in to Watson's room. "What did you do then?" Watson showed him. The current had been unbroken and Bell had heard the whine of the spring.

The miracle was that Bell had recognized his telephone formula in that faint outcry, and had understood that in that moment the telephone had been born. The date was June 2, 1875.

The harmonic was at once abandoned. Watson, sharing Bell's feverish excitement, fashioned dozens of telephone instruments following Bell's designs. Ten months later, he was rewarded by hearing the first sentence transmitted by telephone. "Mr. Watson, come here, I want you!"

The development of the telephone was rapid. Soon, as Watson reports, "the telephone was talking so well that one didn't have to ask the other man to say it over again more than three or four times before one could understand quite well, if the sentences were simple."

Thousands of men and women began flocking to Bell's lecture demonstrations of the new invention. It was astonishing enough to hear English speech issue from what looked like the cover of an ordinary sewing machine. Most astounding, however, was the ability of the telephone to speak in any language. When the Emperor of Brazil heard it, he exclaimed, "My God! It talks!" The treat of every performance was Watson's bellowing from some point miles away such songs as "Hold the fort!" and "Do not trust him, gentle lady." The voice came into the hall, cracked, faint and fading. But it came!

New York City heard this strange performance for the first time on May 11, 1877—and demanded more. Bell offered to sell the invention to Western Union for one hundred thousand dollars, but the Company was at the moment as incapable of seeing a profitable future for the telephone, as Congress had earlier been of seeing the tremendous usefulness of the telegraph. Thereupon, two businessmen formed the Telephone Company of New York. After about a year, these men stepped out and the company was reorganized as the Bell Telephone Company of New York.

Western Union now began to wonder if it hadn't made a mistake in refusing Bell's offer. It thereupon began a telephone service of its own with an instrument invented by Edison. For a while, New York City had two competing telephone systems. There were then of course few telephone subscribers. But imagine the City today divided between two telephone companies fighting each other! Each subscriber would need two telephones and two sets of directories and more patience than a pup waiting for a cat to fall out of a tree.

However, Western Union soon admitted Bell's rights and signed an agreement leaving the telephone field to the National Bell Telephone Company. The New York Company reorganized several times in the next few years, each time undertaking to serve a larger area. In 1896, it became the New York Telephone Company, responsible for telephone service to a large part of the State of New York.

In much the same way, the many small agencies that had paid for the right to rent out Bell's telephones in their cities and towns, grew up, expanded and combined until in every community or region of the U.S. there was a company to provide for its telephone needs.

Today, the Bell System comprises twenty-one of these regional companies. The twenty-two and a half million telephones of their local lines are tied into a national and international telephone network by the long distance lines of their parent company, the American Telephone and Telegraph Company. The five and a half million telephones of the six thousand operating companies which have sprung up since Bell's patents expired and which are independent of the Bell System, are also connected into the Bell System by the A T & T lines. Thus it is possible for nearly all the millions of telephone subscribers in the U.S. to speak to each other and also to be connected with most of the 26,300,000 telephones in the rest of the world.

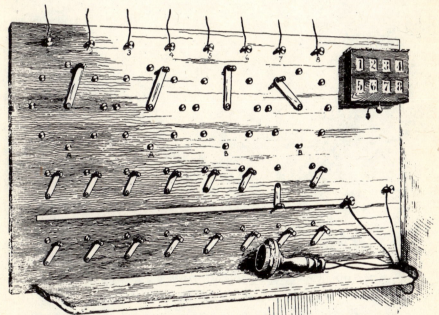

FIRST TELEPHONE SWITCHBOARD INSTALLED IN NEW HAVEN CONN. PROVIDING FOR EIGHT SUBSCRIBERS LINES. 1878.

Watson's employer, Charles Williams, Jr., was the first to string his shop and home together, a distance of three miles between Boston and Somerville, Mass. This was in April, 1877. A month later, the first pair of telephones actually rented for business purposes were connected by one iron wire and a ground—and the telephone earned its first income. Soon after, the number of subscribers increased; but there was as yet no way of interconnecting the telephones of different users.

E. T. Holmes, wishing "to show the telephone to Boston" devised the first switchboard that made it possible for one telephone subscriber to speak to any other subscriber. For two weeks, he connected five banking firms to the switchboard at the Holmes Burglar Alarm Building. The banks used the telephones during the day and were switched to the burglar alarm telegraph during the night.

By the time the telephone company was ready to do business in New York City, a number of communities already had central offices and switchboards. New Haven, Conn., led the way commercially with a board serving eight lines and twenty-one subscribers. At first boys were engaged as telephone operators, but since their good manners as well as their voices often cracked, young women soon took their places.

For some years, telephone conversation required stout lungs. It was "Ahoy! Hoy!" in those days, instead of "Hello." Indeed, Watson tells a joke in which all the farmers waiting in a country grocery "rush out and hold their horses when they see anyone preparing to use the telephone." A central office during a rush hour may well have sounded like a hog calling contest on an Iowa farm.

However, the telephone development never stood still for a moment. The transmitter and the receiver were constantly improved. The lead-sheathed cable came into use, making possible a telephone bridge under the Hudson River between New York and New Jersey. Hand-drawn copper wire replaced the iron wire. It not only was rust-proof, it was a better conductor. In 1884, it enabled New York City to speak to Boston, 235 miles away. The circuit of a single wire with ground return was now a circuit of two insulated wires twisted together. The twisting helped to eliminate disturbances caused by roaming electricity jumping on to one wire and overbalancing it in relation to the other. Twisting maintained the balance in the circuit.

Gradually, speaking over the telephone became less and less of an ordeal. However, by 1892, when New York City and Chicago were first connected by an overhead circuit, New York City had less than fourteen thousand telephone subscribers in a population of two million five hundred thousand. Only about ten percent of the businessmen had installed the service. The rest were mainly discouraged by the high rate, a flat $240 a year.

In 1894, with the introduction of the message rate plan, the Company was able to cut the rate to one hundred and twenty dollars a year for seven hundred telephone messages or seventeen cents each. Five years later, the rate was down to twelve and a half cents a call. The telephone now began to enter well-to-do homes. Few business concerns could do without it. Even the neighborhood grocer, butcher and baker found it increased their business and saved them a great deal of time. Between 1900 and 1920 when the city was doubling its population, the number of telephone subscribers was multiplied fifteen times.

The telephone speaking qualities over reasonably short distances became almost as good as they are today. Its range was more than doubled by highly magnetic loading coils that pepped up the fading electric energy every six thousand feet. In 1911, New York City and Denver spoke over a direct overhead line. In 1913, Salt Lake City, twenty-six hundred miles away was brought into the eastern metropolis. Two years later, San Francisco entered its conversational circle.

This territorial conquest by telephone was of tremendous importance. But perhaps every bit as important was the fact that the local rate from a public telephone had dropped to a nickel. That nickel rate placed the telephone within everyone's reach. It made it the most democratic and friendly of modern inventions. Those people who could not afford the service in their homes welcomed the coin box at the corner drug store.

New York City, with twice as many telephones as London and more telephones than in all of France, averages about ten million conversations a day, half a million to points outside its boundaries. It is served by 164 central offices housing about 195 centrals. Furthermore, it has over twenty-eight thousand private switchboards, called PBX boards, which employ several times as many telephone operators as are employed in the central offices. The PBX operators handle over half the calls in the city. The PBX board in the main office building of the Consolidated Edison Company at times has thirty thousand conversations a day pouring through it.

Lower Manhattan is of course the busiest telephone area in the city. Within this region's skyscrapers are housed the business agents of almost every large-scale business concern in the country. Its financial district draws in most of the available money in the country and distributes it wherever in the world it will make a profit. It is the country's fair grounds for imports and exports, for food, clothing, jewelry, entertainment and a thousand other commodities. During business hours, its population trebles. For these reasons it is the most concentrated telephone traffic center in the world.

Let us make a few calls and trace the course of the invisible electrons from the moment they leap into action in our transmitter to the moment their energy causes sound waves in the distant receiver.

Nearly ninety-five percent of New York City's telephones are dial instruments. Nevertheless, our first call will be from a manual instrument. After all, about two-fifths of the telephones of the United States end at manual switchboards where operators make all connections.

Your number, let us say, is MUrray Hill 3-1597. That means that the wires entering your telephone begin at the telephone central office MUrray Hill 3.

The moment you lift the receiver off the hook, an electric circuit is closed.  Thereupon the electrons flash through your wires out of the house, under the sidewalk and into the cable which takes them to the cable vault of your central office.  Still faithful to your circuit, though there may be as many as 2,121 pairs of wires packed tightly together with it in your 2⅝ inch lead-covered cable, the electrons tumble out of the vault and into the telephone building to a connection on what is called the main frame.

All telephone wires coming into the building enter by way of the main frame.  This is an orderly maze of connections, some thousands of which are to subscribers' lines, other thousands are to spare lines which can be enlisted in any emergency, and some hundreds are to other central offices.

Behind the main frame is the intermediate frame which looks very much like the first frame.  It is called the intermediate because it is the intermediary or the ambassador between the connections on the main frame and the connections on the frame of the manual switchboard.  Your electrons therefore skip to the intermediate frame and up to the switchboard frame where they light a tiny lamp in order to call the operator's attention to their presence.

Switchboards have kept pace with telephone development in the direction of speed and efficiency. The basic idea of the multiple switchboard was first put into operation in Chicago in 1879. In this case, it meant that each subscriber's line ending at the switchboard's frame was connected to two duplicate sections of the switchboard. Thus two operators saw the flash of each incoming call and one or the other hastened to answer it.

On a modern multiple switchboard, each subscriber line that terminates at the switchboard is duplicated or "multiplied" on every section of the board. Thus, a board equipped to serve six thousand subscriber lines and consisting of twenty sections, has twenty times six thousand or one hundred and twenty thousand points of connection. There is rarely any waiting for an operator's reply.

Even with dial service, many operators are needed to handle out-of-town calls and other calls requiring special assistance. So the great dial central offices of the City are supplemented by large multiple manual boards, though these differ in some important details of operation from those used for manual service alone.

The moment your electrons flash their signal on the multiple sections of a manual switchboard, one of the operators plugs a cord into your connection. Immediately the light signal goes out. The cord brings your circuit to her telephone head-set as soon as she presses a knob or listening key on the desk before her.

"Number, please," she says, speaking into the curved horn of the transmitter on her chest.

Many years ago when the telephone was young, you would have replied, "I want to speak to Tom Jones." But many years ago, many things were different. For instance, the instrument the operator is wearing now weighs thirteen ounces whereas once it was a six pound load. The latest type of operator's set is even lighter and has a transmitter that follows the operator's lips as she turns her head.

And how quiet the office is! It is like a strange library where the librarians sit before their shelves and silently reach for the conversations which their invisible public desires.

Today, you give the number of the person with whom you wish to converse. If it has the same central designation as yours, its connection is clearly marked on the switchboard. The operator has only to plug into it the other end of the cord already plugged into your connection. Before she does so, however, she must be certain that Tom's circuit is not being used at the moment. She therefore touches the tip of the metal plug of the cord to the rim of the line for Tom's connection. If his line is busy, she knows it by a warning click in her head phone. If there are no clicks, she plugs in. A signal lamp at Tom's switchboard connection lights.

Now your electrons tumble into Tom's circuit down to the intermediate frame, across to the main frame, into the cable that takes them under the streets to Tom's house and into the small black box to which his telephone is attached. The operator sets the bells in the box to ringing. When Tom lifts the receiver, the circuit between your instruments is complete and you may now worry the electrons into any sounds or conversation you wish. The operator knows that the call is completed when Tom's signal lamp goes out.

If Tom has a different central office than yours, your operator tests his central's trunk lines with her plug, finds one that is free and plugs into it. When his operator answers and is given Tom's number, she makes the final tie-up of your circuit to Tom. Probably no more than twenty seconds have elapsed between the time you lifted your receiver and the first ring in Tom's telephone box.

The moment Tom's receiver is lifted, a meter attached to your line registers the call. This meter will be photographed at the end of the month and you will be billed accordingly.

While you and Tom are conversing, let's watch the electrons as they carry the sounds back and forth. You are speaking normally, perhaps you are even whispering, nevertheless Tom hears you. The present perfection of the transmitter is the result of a hundred evolutions; the modern receiver has seventy ancestors. Yet fundamentally they remain true to Bell's ideas.

In 1881, an Englishman, Henry Hunning, patented the first important improvement in the transmitter. Nine years later a Bell engineer, Anthony C. White, succeeded in making Hunning's idea practical. Without question, White's contribution, by making speech clearer and easier, helped put the telephone on the road to popularity. His design is the basis of the instrument you and Tom are using.

The modern transmitter has two important parts, a disc of iron called the diaphragm, and the button, a chamber directly behind the diaphragm containing fine grains of carbon. When the sound waves of your voice enter the transmitter, they strike the diaphragm which thereupon vibrates in and out. As a wave bends it in, the diaphragm pushes up against the carbon grains. The more it crowds these electrified grains together, the more the electrons are able to cross from one grain to another and the greater the surge of current over the circuit to Tom. The strength of the current therefore varies with the energy of the sound waves on the diaphragm, just as Bell predicted.

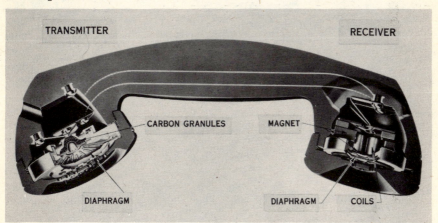

The receiver also has two parts, a magnetic diaphragm and a core of iron alloy, called permalloy, with a wire coil about it. When the current enters the wire coil, the core becomes magnetic and pulls on the diaphragm. The strength with which it pulls is the strength of the current. Thus Tom's receiving diaphragm sets up air waves exactly like the air waves your speech is causing. Tom's ear therefore translates them into your words and tones.

The normal energy of the human voice is astonishingly small. In fact it is so small, that if it were possible to collect the energy of five hundred voices speaking without break for a whole year, that energy would be about sufficient to warm a cup of milk. No wonder Bell and Watson had to roar at each other over the early telephone. The modern transmitter multiplies voice energy one thousand times to the grand total of power that a mosquito can generate.

This power is sufficient to permit normal conversation. But only over a short distance. That is where the circuit loading coils and the vacuum tube amplifiers play their part. Placed at proper intervals along the circuits, they renew the fading energy and send the voice on with its first electrical strength renewed.

The telephone operates on less than one-fiftieth of a watt of direct current. So faint is this power that Bell once completed a telephone circuit through six college professors, whom he persuaded to hold hands. In New York, Edison power lines usually enter a central from opposite sides of the building in order that an accident to one line might not affect the other. Small dynamos convert the alternating current into direct current and charge it into a row of enormous storage batteries. These batteries have an operating capacity of two weeks so that even if Edison power were to fail wholly, telephone communication would not be impaired. Except for ringing and dial tone machines which are on alternating current, the batteries operate all telephone equipment whether dial or manual. A particular advantage of drawing current from the batteries is that the telephone circuits are spared the hum and crackle of generating machinery.

Suppose we examine the circuits that carry New York City's daily load of nearly ten million telephone conversations under our heedless feet.

Look down a telephone manhole. It opens into a vault. Cables made of an alloy of lead and antimony enter the vault through a bank of ducts on one side and leave it through the ducts on the opposite wall.

Sitting in the vault is a telephone man splicing two cable ends. A bewildering number of paper-insulated wires fan out of the wrist-thick cable sheaths, each containing as many as 3,636 or even 4,242 wires. How can the man possibly know which wires belong together? After all they are capable of 1,620,000 or more conversational combinations. Suppose he mixed them up!

But he doesn't. The wires are divided into eighteen groups, each insulated in its own color. The cable man works on one group at a time. He touches two circuit ends together. If they belong together he will get a buzzer signal from his co-worker stationed at the other end of the cables.

When all the circuits are spliced, the cable men will enclose them in a moisture-proof lead sleeve and then solder the sleeve to the cable sheath in much the same way as the telegraph cable worker. Both are worried about moisture and both take much the same measures to defeat it.

The development of the cable was difficult and slow. Indeed, too slow for the patience of the people in large cities who had to live under the shadow of countless wires borne aloft by unsightly forests of poles. In New York City, this aerial congestion of telephone, telegraph and power lines finally led to a revolt. On April 16, 1889, under the orders of Mayor Hugh J. Grant, a crew of men climbed the ninety foot poles at the corner of Broadway and 14th Street, and sheared the lines to the ground, in protest against the dangerous mess of wires downed in that winter's famous blizzard. Thousands came to cheer this dramatic demand for an open and safe sky.

However, the problem the telephone engineers faced could not be solved by public anger. Underground cables carried sound only one-thirtieth of the distance of open wire circuits; they sheathed only fifty circuits and cost about $155 per mile of circuit to install; and they had to be put into the underground vaults and ducts of the Consolidated Telegraph and Electric Subway Company, which had the sole right to dig up the streets of the city. When

laid in these vaults, the telephone circuits became noisy with the electricity they absorbed from the neighboring power lines.

The City solved this last difficulty by chartering the Empire City Subway Company and giving it the sole right to build and lease vaults and ducts for the use of all the communications services. The telephone engineers gradually found the answers to the other two difficulties. By 1895, most of the wires in the business sections were below streets. By 1928, installed cable cost per mile of circuit, including the ducts, was down to ten dollars. Today, scarcely any open wire remains within city limits.

Getting back to your phone call, what happens if you dial it? Your connection is then made mechanically instead of manually. Hundreds of small electromagnets cause hundreds of small switches or relays to perform several hundred actions all of which together take no more time than an operator would take and are even more accurate.

Experimentation with automatic controls began in 1879. However, not until World War I ended did the Bell System feel that it had solved the problem so far as meeting the service requirements of a large city was concerned. In 1922, it put into operation New York City's first dial central office, Pennsylvania.

Here's how the dial equipment gets your number. When you lift the receiver, a switch in the instrument closes the circuit to your central office. But instead of the current lighting a lamp on a switchboard, it passes from the main and intermediate frames to your connection on what is called the finder frame. Here, as with the multiple switchboard where there are a number of operators to do your bidding, there are a number of metal fingers any one of which can find your live circuit and tie into it.

This tie-in goes to two places, to a whirring motor which gives you the dial tone you hear meaning "go ahead," and to the sender frame where the number you now begin dialing is set up by switches on seven circular discs.

If the number, we'll say UNiversity 4-8099, is within your own telephone central, the first disc will turn to U, the second to N, the third to 4. At once you will be connected to the office distributing frame. This frame is divided into four sections: thousands, hundreds, tens and units, and each section responds to the movements of the discs on the sender frame. As you dial 8099, and the discs set it up, a metal finger glides up the thousand section of the distributing frame until it finds a free 8; a finger in the hundred section finds a free 0; a finger in the ten section contacts a free 9; and finally, the unit finger moves to grip the only possible unit 9 on the frame. You are now on the 8099 circuit. A ringing machine, which operates with the dial tone as one compact unit, rings your friend's telephone. When he answers it, the circuit between you is complete, and the call is automatically registered on your meter.

If the number you are calling is in another central, BArclay 7, perhaps, the UNiversity 4 sender selects a free wire to Barclay 7. The rest of the number is then set up on the Barclay 7 sender and distributing frames.

Dial calls to manual telephones are connected to the switchboard at the manual office. Here the called number appears on the switchboard in illuminated figures and is completed by the operator. Manual calls to dial offices are completed by dial operators on switchboards that have numbered keys instead of cords. The operator completes the call by depressing the proper keys.

If this explanation seems a bit difficult to follow, console yourself with the fact that no one telephone engineer is master of the almost nine hundred mechanical operations that take place between the simple acts of lifting two dial receivers. And if in this world of electromagnets, switches and metal fingers, you have so far missed the human touch, be assured that it takes a small army of telephone men to service it. Besides, dial centrals are incomplete without manual switchboards and girl operators. Blind people prefer to dial Operator and let her get the number they want. People have also to be helped with wrong numbers, changed numbers and other forms of information.

And now, suppose you wish to make a call outside but near the city. Your central office operator, if she does not have direct circuits to the point, will set up a connection with one of two tandem offices. A tandem office is a central office for other central offices.

If your party lives on the fringe of Manhattan or in nearby New Jersey, your call will probably be routed through Metropolitan tandem which will then connect you with the telephone central from which your friend's telephone is served. If he lives in a more distant suburb, then your call will go through Suburban Tandem. This office has cables to about one hundred and fifty suburban offices.

Both tandem offices have automatic equipment. Calls through Suburban Tandem arrive at the central office you are calling as numbers on an electrical display plate. In some cases, the number is repeated by a voice film which speaks it into the ear of the completing operator. This is an example of modern magic which has learned to change sound into light and light into sound. One of the other marvels at Suburban is a trouble-shooting machine which automatically types a report if any difficulty arises in completing your call.

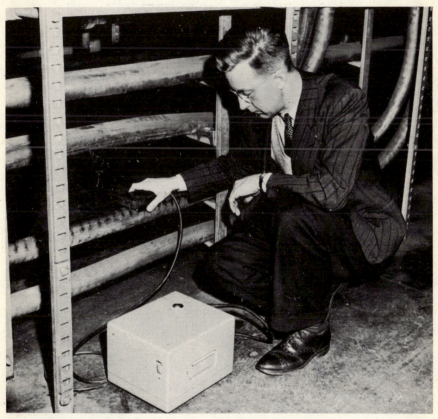

Possibly the most interesting group of telephone centrals is operated by AT&T in the Long Distance Building at 32 Sixth Avenue, the avenue which Mayor LaGuardia, in a pixie moment, renamed the Avenue of the Americas. The building houses the largest and busiest long distance office in the world.

The block-long manual switchboard of Long Distance is like the center of a spider's web. From it radiate some six thousand direct circuits to important cities in the United States, Canada, Mexico and Cuba. The average pre-war time between the lifting of the receiver at the center and any other on this maze of wire paths was under two minutes. We may be sure that with the added equipment made possible by peace-time conditions, this speed of service will be surpassed.

Often calls that do not originate or end at the center are nevertheless routed through its two hundred cables. Through this center also flows the voice traffic passing by radiotelephone to and from many overseas points and, in normal times, to and from ships at sea.

Seated at another switchboard in the building are about eighty operators serving "TWX," the code initials for Teletypwriter Exchange Service. The teletypwriter is the telephone name for the teleprinter.

If you lease one of the 17,247 teletypwriters connected to TWX switchboard, you may communicate with any of the other teletypwriters. Starting your machine lights a lamp on the TWX switchboard. An operator will then plug in and type OPR, meaning "operator at your service." When you have typed the number you are calling, she will answer, O.K., and plug into the line to the exchange you want and repeat the number to the TWX operator there. This operator will make the final connection. A moment later you may click away to your heart's content.

There is also private line teletypewriter service. In this service, direct lines connect two or more machines for writing by wire, as for example between the main and branch offices or plants of a business concern. Many New York Stock Exchange houses have private wire systems, some of which cover the country. The major press associations are among the largest users of private line service. In addition to private line teletypewriter service, they lease private line telephone and Morse telegraph circuits and special channels for the transmission of pictures. Altogether, more than one and a half million miles of private networks are leased by the press, the government and business corporations.

Communications over a private wire network using seventeen thousand miles of permanent specially equipped circuits enter your home every day without your being aware of their telephone roots. The web unites the member stations of the four coast-to-coast broadcasting networks and the many regional networks. Some day, radio relay systems, now in the experimental stage, may make it possible to pluck network programs out of the air. At present, however, radio stations cannot select chain programs out of the confused air and transmit them to you clearly. Besides, the radio station in which the program originates would have to have much more powerful and expensive equipment if it wished to send its program widely. The telephone circuits solve both these problems.

The principal control points in the system of chain broadcasting are the long distance offices in New York, Chicago, Denver and Los Angeles. These and subsidiary control and switching offices permit any desired combinations of stations and quick hookups from one station to another nationally or regionally. Since New York City is the heart of the studio programming of the larger networks, the control room in the Long Distance Building in New York is a mighty busy place. Here a score of technicians assemble the stations of the network which are scheduled to receive any particular program at a second's interval, split them into a dozen separate little chains, and as quickly reassemble them into one listening unit again. In this office, also, are probably the champion radio listeners of the world. As the program comes into their ear phones, perhaps faint with distance, they rub out its noises and send it out again fresh and amplified. Sometimes, when circuit trouble develops, these guardians of the air waves reroute the program through other channels. And not a single listener is the wiser! How many serve us of whose services we are unaware!

To a very real extent, long distance lines are the vital threads of the country's life. They must at all costs be protected against injury or interruption. Just as the blizzard of 1888 helped to arouse people to demand the burying of local wires, so another destructive storm in 1909 caused the head of AT&T to order long distance cables underground. That storm carried away the overhead telephone circuits through which the New York City press was expecting to hear the eyewitness accounts of the inauguration of a new President of the United States, William H. Taft.

At that period, underground cables could convey speech a distance of about ninety miles. However, the further development of the loading coil or repeater to pep up the dying current, helped the Bell engineers to extend this performance. Four years later, they were able to complete an underground cable between Boston and Washington.

In 1915, thanks to the amplifying powers of the DeForest vacuum radio tube, circuit performance both underground and overhead was tremendously improved. In that year the tubes made possible the first transcontinental conversation, Boston to San Francisco. Since then, three more transcontinental lines have been built and a fifth is now being constructed. The tubes are used only on long lines and are installed in repeater stations between 5 and 50 miles apart, depending on the type of carrier system installed.

Nearly forty thousand tubes stud the repeaters and testing equipment used in the Long Distance Building in New York.

The work of putting cables underground is still continuing.

Where possible a specially designed plow is used to plow the cable under. Sixty percent of the country's long distance cables are today safely below ground.

Of 148 cables linking Manhattan with the general system, forty-eight are toll and long distance cables. Of these, about forty pass under the surrounding waterways by way of railway and vehicular tunnels and under the Harlem River through a special cable tunnel built in 1931 and lying twenty-seven feet below the low-tide level.

Telephone circuit advance still continues. Long distance lines use carrier current in the same way as the telegraph.

Perhaps one of the most baffling circuits which the Bell engineers have developed is the phantom circuit. It is a circuit that has no wires of its own. It uses the wires of one telephone circuit as one of its wires and the wires of a second circuit as the return wire. Specially built repeating coils make the connection between these two borrowed circuits. The phantom circuit rises between them like a disembodied spirit at a seance where everyone is holding hands. Thus are three circuits created where before there were only two.

The idea of the phantom circuit first occurred in 1883, but was not successfully applied until twenty years later. Since then, nearly one-seventh of the long lines of the country have been made available for phantom operation.

Another great advance only recently announced and known as the rural power line carrier system, permits the transmission of both electric power and telephone conversations over the same line at the same time. This is designed for use in rural areas that have power lines but no telephone lines.

The latest development in cables is the coaxial cable. The most advanced coaxial cable contains four coaxial units, each pair of which can handle 480 two-way conversations going at the same time and without interference from any of the others. The coaxial units are flexible copper tubes or pipes with a thick wire inside each. Their circuits are based on the radio principle of different wave lengths.

The coaxial cable is, of course, best known for its development as a television circuit. New York City has two coaxial cable television circuits, one between NBC studios in Radio City and the

Empire State Building, and the other between the Grand Central Building and the Chrysler Building. A new coaxial cable route now connects Washington, D.C., Philadelphia and New York in long distance telecasting. Bell engineers are surely developing the most amazing stage of distance communication, the stage wherein we will not only speak with distant friends but see them.

Within the next five years, the Bell System will install coaxial cables along the Dallas-Los Angeles route and many other routes comprising a national coaxial network of about seven thousand miles which will carry both long distance telephone traffic and television programs.

Perhaps there is no more exciting corner in the telephone world than the overseas switchboard at 32 Avenue of the Americas. Not only can its operators connect you to almost any telephone on earth, but they can also channel your voice to a great many vessels at sea. Indeed, their switchboard is the magic carpet which can set you down in Paris, in Cairo, in Santiago or in a cabin of a ship rolling between sea and sky, and do so within the space of a few minutes. There are such magic carpets at San Francisco and at Miami, but two-thirds of the transoceanic connections are made at the New York overseas center. In all, forty-two overseas circuits terminate at New York.

If you were speaking across the Atlantic, your voice would flow from Overseas switchboard in the Long Distance Building to the Overseas control room in that building. Here apparatus would build it up or tone it down. If it were being transmitted to London, it might go by short wave or by one of two long wave circuits. If by long wave, your voice would continue by cable to the radio station at Rocky Point, Long Island, where it would be cast out into space. Your distant friend's voice would be received at the station at Houlton, Maine, and proceed by overland circuit to you. If your conversation were by short wave, the transmitters at Lawrenceville or Ocean Gate, N. J., would be used to send your voice out, and one of the short wave receiving stations at either Manahawkin or Netcong, N. J., would bring your friend's voice in. Long wave is subject to static but is less disturbed by magnetic storms. Short wave, on the other hand, is scattered by a magnetic storm but is safe from static. Between the two, transatlantic conversations seldom break down. The only long wave circuits today are on the London route.

Perhaps, you have been wondering how it is possible to carry on a private conversation when it is exploded into the universe. Why can't anyone with a good radio set pick it up? The answer is that he can, but he wouldn't understand it. Translate this, if you can: "Noyl hob e ylippey ylond." It is only "Mary had a little lamb," but it is scrambled. The second line of that famous verse goes like this: "Heez fludes yes yout oz sway."

To insure privacy, radio telephony scrambles sounds and pitches though it does not alter volume. Over it a mouse would speak with the bass voice of a lion, while the lion would be half frightened to death to hear his deep thunder reduced to a falsetto squeak. However, this "cryptic" or scrambled speech is unscrambled by automatic devices at the control office and neither telephone user is aware of the impish distortion his words have undergone.

Young Watson quit Bell Telephone in 1881. He had always wanted to build ships. He now did so. Later he even built battleships. The young Scotch immigrant, Alexander Bell, also quit soon after. His new interest was in the possibility of flying machines, and in time he succeeded in advancing man's mastery of the air. However, the telephone, though abandoned by its first inventors, did not stop growing, as you well know.

Its development had, in any case, become too complex for any two men. It needed to be nursed along by a growing number of scientists, inventors and engineers each devoted to one of its many phases and yet all working together. This collective research and development task was immensely expedited by the establishment of the Bell Telephone Laboratories.

In this splendidly equipped organization Bell and Watson have been multiplied a thousand times. Their work on the telephone has thus never ceased. Indeed, it moves forward every day toward a perfection that no one can foresee. It is in good hands.

# PART V

## HELP! FIRE! POLICE!

## Chapter 12

## Help! Fire!

"Three o'clock! And all is well!"

The cry of the watchman echoes through the frosty night of New Amsterdam. The good burghers sleeping in nightcaps, their feet against hot stones, stir—and immediately fall asleep more soundly. "All is well." The stout watchman flails his arms across his chest. It is hard to keep warm.

Suddenly, he stares up at Peter Koven's house. Huge, bright cinders are leaping out of the chimney. The wind blots out some of them, but many sparks are falling upon the wooden tiles of the roof. He notices a gray wisp of smoke. A moment later, a tile thrusts out a tongue of flame.

Fire! Fire! Fire!

Furiously, he knocks up Peter and his family.

Fire! Fire!

The fearful cry is taken up by others. In time the fire bell adds its alarm. Citizens know at once where the fire is. They see its glare in the sky. Everyone runs toward it. Some seize the leather buckets which each householder must by law fill and put out on his doorstep for just this sort of emergency. But the water is frozen fast. The eight volunteer firemen arrive with their equipment: 250 buckets. Men and women form a chain between the nearest well and Peter's house. The ice in the well is finally broken. The buckets are dipped, passed from hand to hand, and splashed at the burning house.

But a splash of water has no force; neither can it be thrown very far. In any case it comes too late to save Peter's home. His neighbors are helpless before the hunger of the fire demon.

Not till 1731 did the city's volunteers see a pumping wagon. Two pumpers arrived from England. They were hand-drawn and hand-pumped. The tanks under the pumps had to be filled by bucket. A hand-drawn hose cart ran with each pumper. The new fire equipment was crude, but at least, it was able to throw a stream of water—when there was water.

But you remember, there was not enough water until more than a hundred years later. In the meantime, the hand-pumpers became more powerful. They were built with a double set of seesaw pumps. The lower pump was operated by men standing on the ground; the upper pump was worked by men standing on the wagon deck.

It was not until the first Croton water poured into the reservoir at Fifth Avenue and 42nd Street that the firemen stoked their first steam pumper. This was a fire box and boiler erect on wheels. The firemen did not like it. In fact, they successfully fought against its wider use until 1861.

The City had now both water and the pressure supplied by the steam engines. However, it still lacked a rapid signal system and firemen who would work at their job.

The volunteer fire companies had become social and political clubs that only played at fire fighting. They vied with each other in grandeur of uniform, in dances and in sporting contests. When the fire bell rang, they ran to the engine house, scrambled into uniforms, and when enough of the company were assembled, grabbed the wagon tongues of the pumper and the hose cart and raced to the fire. Sometimes they stopped to fight another company for the honor of being the first to arrive. Reaching the fire, by now crackling merrily, they might be unable to locate the hydrant because somebody from a company still on its way had put a barrel over the hydrant so that his company would be the first after all.

Unfortunately, the fire never waited until this sporting contest was decided.

Finally, in 1865, the fire insurance companies and the long-suffering public forced the City to establish a paid, professional fire department. Along with the outraged volunteers, went all the hand-pumpers and hand-drawn vehicles. The steam pumper came into its own as did the huge, high-spirited horses that now drew all apparatus.

The volunteer firemen had also prevented the City from trying out the electric fire alarm box and telegraph signal system already in use in Boston, Philadelphia, Baltimore and New Orleans. They were well pleased with the fire towers from which watchmen, spying the fire, sounded the number of the district on the tower bells. Four years after the volunteers had had their last say, the new Fire Department began to respond to alarms that came to the company houses electrically. The towers were gradually abandoned.

Today you may see one of the old towers in Mount Morris Park in Manhattan. Its bells, long silent, clanged the alarm for the last time in 1888, when the great blizzard had blown down the poles which bore the wires of the alarm system.

Curiously enough, there are still districts within the City which have no fire boxes. Governors Island which once used to report a fire by shooting a cannon, now telephones the Central Office of the Fire Alarm Telegraph Bureau. Bedloe's Island telephones, and Ellis Island blows a siren and telephones.

In 1908, the high pressure water systems constructed by the Department of Water Supply, Gas and Electricity, added a most effective weapon against fire. The following year, the Fire Department began motorizing its apparatus, and by 1922 the last of its spirited horses had disappeared from the City's streets. When the picturesque steam engine was displaced by the vastly more powerful and more efficient pump of the gasoline motor in the automobile engines, the New York City Fire Department became one of the best fire-fighting units anywhere.

The City has three high pressure zones each with its own system of mains and pumping stations. The first protects Manhattan below 34th Street where the skyscrapers, the civic center, the great wholesale markets, the docks and the teeming East Side tenements form the most congested and most valuable area in the world. The second zone protects the docks as well as the civic, business and hotel center of Brooklyn. The third zone is in Coney Island, which because of its crowded wooden structures, has had a history of rapidly spreading fires.

There is a fourth zone which covers the Brooklyn Navy Yard. This was built by the United States Government. It too is complete with high pressure mains and a pumping station. The system is connected to the Brooklyn high pressure main, so that, should the station break down, the valve separating the two systems can be lifted to permit the Brooklyn station to furnish water at high pressure.

The high pressure mains are separate and apart from the mains carrying drinking water. They are placed on the opposite side of the street. You can recognize the high pressure system by the heavy hydrants with four outlets for hose connection. The hydrants of the low pressure mains have only two outlets.

Each of the two Manhattan pumping stations can get its water from three separate sources: Croton water through a thirty-six-inch-wide main from the Central Park reservoir; if that fails, Catskill water from a riser shaft in City Tunnel No. 1; if that fails, river water through a thirty-six-inch main.

Brooklyn's two stations can get their water from City Tunnel No. 1 and from the harbor. However, since salt water is harmful to merchandise, Brooklyn and Manhattan would use it only if the fresh water supply were to fail. Coney Island's single station uses both salt and fresh water together. The trunk mains that convey the water from the stations to the street are twenty and twenty-four inches in diameter. From these mains, the water is brought to the hydrant by eight-inch pipes.

As you can see by the map of Manhattan zone, it is divided into three parts, so that, should one section break down, the other two can still function. The stations each have six eight hundred horse-power pumps. One pump in either station raises the water pressure throughout the whole system. The normal pressure in the mains is about thirty-five pounds to the square inch. The pumps are able to increase that pressure to three hundred pounds. However, firemen usually call for pressure under two hundred pounds, a force sufficient to shoot a rigid stream of water fourteen stories high.

Pressure is applied by one pump at a time. If the fire is in the area above Canal Street, the Gansevoort Station starts the first pump. As more pressure is needed, it puts the second and third pumps to work. If still more pressure is needed, the Oliver Street station follows with three of its pumps, the Gansevoort adds the rest of its pumps, and the Oliver Street Station brings its last three into play. If the fire is below Canal Street, the stations operate in reverse order. The twelve pumps working together can supply about fifty thousand gallons per minute at one hundred and fifty pounds pressure.

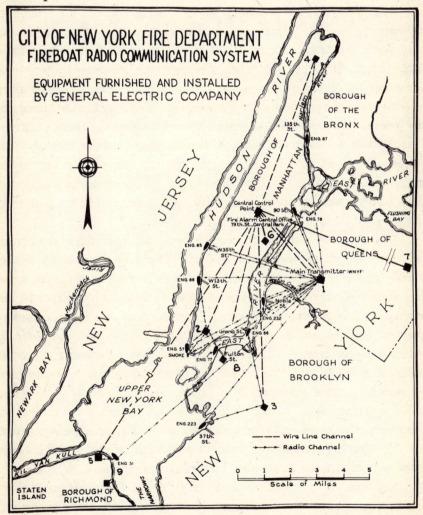

However, only once were as many as eleven pumps required. That was during the famous Three-Cornered Night, half a year after the high pressure system was completed. Fires raged in three widely separated points in lower Manhattan: one, a four-alarm explosion in the wholesale grocery district; the second, a three-alarm blaze in a Bowery factory; the third, a five-alarm conflagration in a Broadway building. Over a hundred pieces of apparatus, some from Brooklyn, gathered to fight these fires. Of these, only the fifty steam pumpers were idle. They had as usual, connected to the low pressure pumps—but only to be ready in the event of a breakdown in the high pressure system. The system did not fail. That night tested the system almost to capacity and proved its worth.

There have been occasions since then, when one or the other sections of the Manhattan zone had to be shut off. Once and once only were the two sections at the tip of the island damaged at the same time. It happened while the Seventh Avenue subway was constructing its tunnel across the East River. A landslide at Fulton Street smashed the mains of the sections. Worse, it also broke the low pressure mains. While repairs were being made, there occurred a fire. The firemen arrived. What do you suppose they did for water? They attached their hose to the stand pipes leading to the water tanks atop the nearby buildings. The steam engines were then put to work and soon the fire was licked. There is always a way.

The Fire Department regularly checks all hydrants and hydrant valves to see that they are in order. The Department of Water Supply makes all repairs immediately. A broken hydrant or valve may mean greater property damage and even injury to life. In the winter, hydrants may be frozen. A steam device is at once used to thaw it and the resulting water is pumped out so that the hydrant will not again freeze. During the time that a hydrant is out of order, it wears a metal disk to warn engine men not to waste time by attaching their pumpers to it.

Important as is the high pressure water system, powerful as are the pumper engines, as brave and well-trained and well-equipped as are the City's firemen, the Fire Department would yet be fairly helpless without the Bureau of Fire Alarm Telegraph.

Suppose you were to sit on a hot stove, and suppose your nervous system failed to notify you that you were being scorched. What would happen? You would burn to death. You would have no way of knowing that you were in danger. As it is, your body is a network of tiny telegraph wires, all connecting with a conduit in your spine and finally ending in your brain. In case of danger, a nerve immediately notifies your brain and the brain at once sends the correct order to the proper nerve or nerves leading to that part of your body which must act in order to save you. The speed of these messages is what protects you from many a serious accident.

The Bureau of Fire Alarm Telegraph is the nervous system of the Fire Department. Its brain is the Central Office in each Borough from which the nerves branch out to every part of that Borough. The red fire alarm box is one of the touchy ends of one of these nerves. Pull down the lever of the box and immediately the brain has been warned and is sending out along other nerves the proper messages for action. In twenty to thirty seconds, the fire companies know where to go. If the fire is in a high pressure zone, the pumps are at work within the minute. A few minutes later, the firemen are at the scene of the fire. Every second is precious. Fire spreads with amazing rapidity. A few minutes delay may mean the destruction of a whole city block. In this terrifying truth lies the importance of the fire alarm telegraph system.

Exactly how does the system work?

Let us begin with a Central Office of the Fire Alarm Telegraph Bureau to which all alarms must come and from which all orders must go. Each Borough has its own Central Office, a fireproof building situated in a park and thus safe from any fire in the community. The large signal room has a receiving board on one side and a transmitting or sending apparatus on the other side.

All the fireboxes in the Borough are connected by circuits to the receiving board. A circuit consists of a single wire which begins at the receiving board, is carried either in a tile conduit below the street, or by aerial wire strung between telegraph or telephone poles, makes all the connections assigned to it, and returns to the receiving board. Since any break in that wire will put all its fireboxes out of use, a circuit seldom serves more than twenty boxes. Except in Manhattan and Richmond the circuits are divided into groups of eight. Each group receives electric power from its own motor generator, so that trouble in one group does not affect any other. The circuits in Manhattan have a common source of power.

The pulling of a handle on a fire box sends its number to the receiving board. The number registers by buzz and a flashing light for each tap, and is also written out on a ticker tape. It does this four times. Thus there can be no mistake about it.

Even before the last buzz, the dispatcher at the opposite board has already set the signal which is to go out to all the fire companies in the Borough. The number is checked for accuracy by another dispatcher, a switch is thrown, and the signal speeds to all the company houses in the Borough, ringing first on the primary circuit and again on a secondary circuit. Those companies that have been assigned to answer the first alarm of Box No. 213, for example, roll out. The companies assigned to answer the second alarm hold themselves in readiness.

You notice that the Fire Department provides one or more pinch hitters at all crucial points.

The supply of electricity to the Central Office is triply safe-guarded. The electric light company provides two cables which enter the building from opposite directions. If these cables fail, a huge storage battery automatically goes into action. If the battery fails, a gasoline-driven electric generator provides the required juice. If all these were to break down, there remains the telephone. The life and property of a great city are in the keep of the Fire Department. At no point must it completely fail.

The Central Offices also receive verbal alarms telephoned in by individuals and the special buildings signal alarms telegraphed in by the four private fire alarm protection companies operating in the City. Their privately owned manual alarm boxes are installed a box to every two floors in smaller buildings, a box to a floor in larger buildings. This enables firemen to go at once to the actual scene of the fire. You can imagine the time lost and the consequent damage if firemen were to answer an alarm at the Empire State Building only to have to race through its eighty-five floors and the tower in search of the blaze.

Many loft buildings have mains that lead down from the water tank on the roof and connect with a sprinkler system of narrow pipes hung from the ceilings of the floors. These pipes have many valve heads each sealed with a fusible link which will melt even with a small fire beneath it. The moment the water begins to fountain out of the sprinkler head—the rate is 30 gallons a minute—it sets off an automatic telegraph signal which is received in the central office of the company which installed the service. If the signal comes in during the working day, the company telephones the point of trouble to warn of the overflow and to ask whether the Fire Department is needed. If it is, the company promptly telegraphs the Central Office of the Fire Department. If the overflow occurs at night, the alarm is relayed to the Fire Department without further ado. The dispatchers at the Central Office transmit the signal 5.7 to the nearest engine company and hook and ladder to investigate the alarm. This also does for verbal alarms. If the Chief of Battalion in charge needs more apparatus, he sends a fire alarm from the nearest street fire alarm box.

The oldest and largest private fire alarm protection company in the City and the only one which is national in scope, is the ADT with about twelve thousand fire alarm boxes in New York City buildings or as many as the Fire Department has on the streets. The underground wire systems of the ADT and its competitors are indeed a vital part of the City's defense against fire.

It is night. Except for the scrub women in the skyscrapers, lower Manhattan is deserted. A lonely policeman is patrolling

Whitehall Street. He tries a store door. Suddenly, there is an electric flash above the night light in the store. The light dies. In the darkness, the officer is shocked to see a small flame licking the ceiling.

Racing to the corner, he pulls down the handle of Box 10. As the first buzz sounds in the Central Office in Central Park, the dispatchers take their places.

Tap—Tap Tap Tap Tap Tap Tap Tap Tap Tap Tap

The buzzer, the flashing light, the ticker tape all say 10. A dispatcher has already set 10 on the transmitter. The Chief checks it for accuracy, a switch is thrown—and the alarm for Box 10 at Whitehall and Front Street sounds on the gongs of all the company quarters in Manhattan.

Everywhere men have leaped to their stations ready to go.

"Ten! Whitehall and Front! We roll!" That is the cry in the nearest four engine companies and two hook-and-ladder companies. Two Chiefs of Battalion and the Deputy Chief of Division 1 roll with them.

"Ten! Whitehall and Front! Due on a second alarm!" That is the warning of the watchmen in the neighboring five engine companies, one hook-and-ladder, the Manhattan Rescue Company, the Manhattan Water Tower, and Fire Boat 57.

In all other company quarters in the Borough, the shout is, "Ten! Whitehall and Front! Not for us!"

Even as the trucks roll out into the street, the engineer at the Oliver Street High Pressure Station throws the switch for the first pump. Gansevoort Station will not be called unless four pumps are needed. But it stands by.

In a few minutes the firemen whirl on the scene. The fire has spread to the merchandise. The store is a blazing pocket. It looks like a bad night.

While the hose lines are being attached to the high pressure hydrants, the Deputy Chief in command sends a second alarm from the fire box. Using its Morse key, he taps 2.2—10. 2.2 is the second alarm call. Back comes the signal 2.3, which means: We have received your call.

Two, two-ten! The signal flashes from the transmitter at the Central Office to the company gongs in the Borough. It is also received in the Central Offices of the rest of the City.

"Two, two-ten!" cry the watchmen in the companies assigned to the second alarm at Box 10. "We go!" Out they roll. Fire Boat 57 joins them.

"Two, two-ten! Whitehall and Front! Due on a third alarm!" That is the warning in five engine companies, Fire Boat 77, one hook-and-ladder, and the Borough's Gas and Oil Wagon which may be needed to supply fuel to the engines.

"Not for us!" cry all the other company watchmen.

Back at the scene of the fire, the hose lines have already been stretched to the flaming building. The hose valves are fixed to deliver 100 pounds pressure. At a signal from the hose men, the water is released. It smashes into the fire. The hook-and-ladder men are at work putting up ladders, getting into the building. The fire boats stand by to protect the docks. The gasoline pumpers have attached lines to the low pressure hydrants. They will go into action only if the high pressure system should fail.

As the second alarm assignment speeds to the fire, gongs going and sirens screaming, an automobile driven by a reckless man darts into the path of Engine No. 9. The engine driver swerves his machine. It piles up on the sidewalk. The Commanding Officer, seeing that the engine is disabled, goes at once to the nearest fire box. He sends the signal 13—9. Thirteen is the signal of breakdown for any apparatus. Nine is the number of his engine company. If Hook-and-ladder No. 1 had met with the accident, its signal to Central Office would have been 13—7—1. Seven is the designation of a hook-and-ladder. Following it is the hook-and-ladder company's number.

"Two, three," replies the dispatcher. He must at once send an engine to replace Engine No. 9. He decides to call for Engine Company No. 27. This Company is first due on the third alarm on Box 10. He taps a special call: 5—10—27. The watchman at No. 27 immediately acknowledges the signal by tapping 27. Away goes the engine to take the place of No. 9.

In the meantime, since lower Manhattan is being stripped of fire fighting apparatus, it is important to bring down apparatus to replace it. Another fire in the neighborhood must not be allowed to get a long head start while trucks are being called from distant points in the City. Therefore, as the second alarm detail moves out to the fire, the fire engines and one hook-and-ladder company due on the third alarm move out of their quarters and into the quarters of companies in action.   On arriving, the companies report themselves in service.   Hook-and-Ladder No. 20, which has moved into the quarters of Hook-and-Ladder No. 10, notifies Central Office by tapping the in-service signal, 4.4.4—7—10—20.

Back at the fire, the Commanding Officer sees that it is a real worker.   The flames are roaring up an old shaft.   Fire suddenly blossoms in an adjoining building.   More pressure, more apparatus, more men are needed.   He sends the order to increase the water pressure to 175 pounds, 8—10—175.   Eight is the preliminary signal for the high pressure system.   Then he sends the third alarm call, 3.3—10.

Now the third alarm assignment rolls out to the fight.   The companies assigned to answer a fourth alarm hold themselves in readiness.   Companies assigned to take the place of those at the fire make the change.   The third alarm signal is received and transmitted in the other central offices of the city.   This time, the Central Office has warned all the 368 companies of the Fire Department that a serious blaze is being fought in Manhattan at Box 10. The Borough signal for Manhattan and Bronx is 66; for Brooklyn and Queens, it is 77; for Richmond, it is 88.   Therefore, the signal transmitted in Brooklyn, Queens and Richmond is 66—33—10.

With the additional force, the fire is at last controlled.   As companies can be spared, they return to quarters.   Companies that have occupied other houses return to their own quarters.   As soon as these companies are ready to respond to another alarm, they notify the Central Office.   Engine Company No. 6 taps 4.4.4—6. At Central Office, a dispatcher has been keeping a record of the fire and the forces used in combating it.   When the first alarm came in, he went to the file of assignment cards and took out the card for Box 10.   As alarm succeeded alarm, he recorded the companies that had answered the call, the companies that had replaced them, the disablement of Engine Company No. 9 and the special calling of Engine No. 27.   The fire had been very dangerous.  At the call 6.6.6—10—1, the Department ambulance had raced to the scene.   It too is on the record sheet.   Now as the companies begin to send in their 4.4.4 signals the dispatcher marks them as again in service and ready for action.   Thus Central Office knows at all times what its forces are and where they are.

When the fire is in its washing-down stage, the engines at the low pressure hydrants go to work. The high pressure system is too costly to be used at this point. The Commanding Officer notifies Central Office to shut it off. He taps 8—10. Had the high pressure broken down in Section 2, the breakdown signal would have been 13.13—2. Once more in working order, the glad news would be 9.9.9—2.

In 1945, the Fire Department rolled to 49,767 alarms. Of these, 135 were second alarms, 38 third alarms, 14 fourth alarms, and 3 were fifth alarms. 4.4—10 is the fourth alarm call to Box 10. The fifth alarm is 5.5.—10. With the 5.5 call, Box 10 would have had 26 engines, 6 hook-and-ladders and 2 fire boats. If more had been needed, the Borough call, 6.6—10—23—448 transmitted in Brooklyn, would have sent apparatus racing across the bridges of the East River. The whole lower city would have been rocked with fire companies roaring to the fire, replacing each other, and finally returning.

As you can see, we are a long way off from the startled constable and the frozen leather buckets of New Amsterdam. The New York Fire Department has no superior anywhere in the world. The reason that there are so few alarms above a second alarm is speed of signals, speed of arrival, and plenty of water, pressure and manpower. And yet the Department looks forward to certain improvements.

Approximately fourteen percent of its wires are still strung from poles. During the windstorm of September 18-19, 1938, fully a third of the alarm boxes on the aerial circuits were put out of action. Firemen had to be stationed at these boxes so that they could report fires from the nearest telephone. These circuits need the protection of underground tile conduits.

Another improvement the Department will make when it has sufficient maintenance force, will be to back the gong signals at the company houses with teletype machines which will write the signal out. A long gong signal may take half a minute. The teletype takes a few seconds. And every second is terribly important.

Early in 1938, the ten fire boats and the tender were equipped for radio telephone communication. Few firemen know that in 1912 the fire boat James Duane had experimented with radio telegraph. Now, no matter where the boats may be, they can both receive and send orders. But, of course, the telegraph system remains the most reliable. Radio communication sometimes fails.

The Fire Department is not planning to ask for any more high pressure zones. The reason lies in the powerful pumping engines which they are now buying. As fast as possible, the Department of Water Supply is removing the six-inch mains in congested districts and replacing them with eight-inch mains.

And now, before we move on to the next chapter—here's a warning: Don't mail your letters in the fire box!

In 1945, more than one-third of all the alarms received were false alarms. These shams weakened the forces which should always be ready for a real fight. They endangered the lives of the people on the street. They endangered the speeding firemen. These brave men, facing fire, smoke and tumbling walls, risk their lives daily in the run of duty. In 1945, in a force of about ten thousand men, twelve were killed and over one thousand were injured.

Let's not add in any way to the chances our firemen take. Don't play with fire.

## Chapter 13

## Help! Police!

THE STOREKEEPER TURNS cordially to the two young men who have just entered. "What can I do for you?"

"You can put your hands up!" one of the men barks.

The storekeeper faces a revolver. Hastily, the other thug loots the cash register. The two men spring into a waiting car. Easy money! And no trouble in getting away!

Five minutes later, they are caught.

What is the secret of the speed with which the officers of the law have moved? It is in the telephone and telegraph police wires buried under the streets of the city. It is in the police radio.

The New York City Police Department has an enormously

responsible job. It has to protect the lives and property of the largest and wealthiest community in the world. In the course of a year, it arrests or summons almost a million people.

Don't get the idea that New York City has a million desperate gun-toting outlaws in its midst. Most of the arrests and summonses are for such "crimes" as passing a red light while driving, peddling without a license, disobeying the rules of the Health Department, and generally violating the thousand laws which, though petty, are necessary if millions of people are to live safely together. Of crimes serious enough to be punished by imprisonment in a State institution, the city has less than twenty-five thousand a year.

But that is because the Police Department does its job so well. Modern science and invention have given it all sorts of aids: fingerprint identification, the chemical laboratory, the automobile, the airplane. As important as any of these is the ability to receive an instant alarm and instantly to notify the police force to take action.

Today, the cry for help to Police Headquarters is electric and the orders of Police Headquarters to its men snap underground and crackle through the air as fast as lightning.

New York City has eighty-five police precincts. From these spreads a web tying in about 1,726 street telephone boxes. Each precinct switchboard has five call-box circuits. Each circuit has three, sometimes four, call boxes. The circuits are, therefore, party wires.

If Patrolman Sullivan is reporting, Patrolman Clancy and Miller on the same circuit must wait. Patrolman Sullivan glances at his watch. It is ten minutes to the hour. About time to report. He ambles down the street to a telephone call box marked: TO CALL POLICE USE THIS TELEPHONE. That means that you and I and anyone who needs a policeman is free to use the police telephone.

Patrolman Sullivan does not have to ask Central for a connection, neither does he have to dial. He is on a direct wire to his precinct. He picks up the receiver.

"Hello," answers the policeman at the switchboard.

"Patrolman Sullivan reporting. Post one sixty-nine."

"Right!" The police operator makes a record of the call. Sometimes the sergeant at the precinct has special instructions for Sullivan. Somebody may have telephoned a complaint that needs looking into. A kitten may have crawled under a loose board in the floor. Someone is throwing refuse out of a window. Patrolman Sullivan goes to investigate.

The policeman also uses the call box whenever he wants an ambulance or patrol wagon or wishes to report some emergency. The telephone switchboard operator thereupon relays the call to the proper authorities.

The teletypewriter is one of the most valuable of police aids. Its electric message is printed in duplicate, is absolutely secret and can be received without an attendant at the receiver.

The Police Department has seven teletype sending machines and 102 receivers. Each of the precincts has a receiver connected to its Borough Headquarters. Each Borough Headquarters has a sender and receiver which ties in with Police Headquarters in Manhattan and with the other Borough headquarters. In this way a message can be sent to any single teletypewriter or to a group of machines or to all the machines in the city.

Moreover, New York City Police Headquarters is connected

to the teletypewriter stations in the police headquarters of twelve States: New York, New Jersey, Pennsylvania, Connecticut, Massachusetts, Rhode Island, New Hampshire, Delaware, District of Columbia, Virginia, West Virginia, and Ohio. Other states will be tied into this cooperative system as quickly as they install teletypewriter communication.

Here is how this widespread network moves. A couple of gangsters steal a car, snatch a payroll, and zoom out of sight. Within twenty minutes the teletypewriters of twelve states have spread the alarm. Police radios pick it up and broadcast it to the cruising police cars. Patrolmen learn about it when they telephone their hourly report. The gangsters have matched their wits against an invisible power that has set a very visible host of law enforcement agents in their every path. Their chances of escape are not worth betting on.

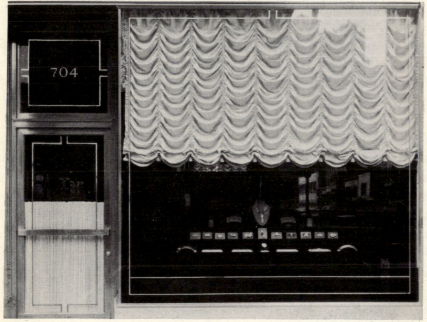

It is two o'clock in the morning. Two men saunter down the deserted street. Suddenly, they vanish into the doorway of a darkened store. While one of them jimmies the door open, the other looks out for trouble. He does not know that trouble started on its way the moment the door was first jarred.

The store is equipped with an electric burglar alarm system

put in by a private company. The alarm system is a closed electric circuit that guards every possible manner of entrance. When the burglar inserted his jimmy and pressed against the door, the circuit was broken. This caused a light to flash on the master panel located at the company's headquarters.

Even before the two burglars enter the store, company headquarters is already plugging in on a direct telephone wire to its branch office nearest to the store and on another direct wire to Police Headquarters. In a moment, company guards and police officers are speeding to the scene.

No, a burglar's lot is not a happy one.

Banks, warehouses, stores, lofts, museums and even some of the wealthier residences are tied in to the burglar alarm system. Some places, especially banks and jewelry shops, have hidden push buttons that can be pressed by an employee in case of a holdup. All alarms come to company headquarters along wires leased from the New York Telephone Company.

Perhaps the best way to measure the value of this simple burglar alarm system is to think of the number of places that a burglar would like to rob in this wealthiest of cities and then to remember that in an entire year, he does not dare break into more than three thousand of them.

Today, the criminal cannot hope to match himself successfully against the officers of the law. The odds against him are too great. When a web of wires hidden four feet or more below the streets of the city can reach up and enmesh his feet, often before he gets away from the scene of the crime, then it is time for him to give up his game.

# PART VI

# TRANSPORTATION

# Chapter 14

## Stop On Red—Go On Green

TWO MILLION MOTORCARS a day stream through the streets of New York City, rocketing across each other's paths and the paths of millions of pedestrians going to and fro about their business or pleasure.

What controls this vast number of individual wills, whether on wheels or heels? What keeps the streets orderly and reasonably safe for passenger and pedestrian? Traffic lights? Yes. But what is behind them? How are they controlled? Who operates them? Where?

Traffic only became a problem in our century. True that, for a brief period before then, the white cotton glove of the policeman had been directing the horse-drawn vehicles at the more congested corners of our big cities. But that was more to prevent fist fights between burly teamsters than to keep their wagons from tangling.

Then came the automobile. People saw the familiar carriage but without a horse. Instead of its front end consuming oats, it consumed gas. It seemed silly.

Ten years later, in 1905, the manufacturers turned out about twenty-five thousand of the unnatural, snorting, rattling, unreliable monsters. Few people thought that motorcars had any future. However, in spite of the fun poked at their product, the manufacturers continued to improve it and to bring its price lower and lower. In 1915, they sold a million cars.

By the time the first World War was over, New York City alone had three-quarters of a million cars jamming its streets. Big cities everywhere were facing a problem new to the history of man: how to keep the traffic rolling swiftly, smoothly, and with the least danger to all concerned.

For some time, the white-gloved hand of the traffic officer continued to operate as a semaphore. It was a simple and easily seen signal. It helped. But not enough. The trouble was that each officer operated his semaphore to suit his own post. Too often the result was a cursing, horn-blowing, siren-screaming bedlam of infuriated drivers smack up against each other and powerless to move. Co-ordination of signals was plainly necessary if traffic conditions were not to become a hopeless snarl. New York City was the first community in the world to attempt this co-ordination.

It began with tall traffic towers erected at the fifty busiest intersections. Each avenue had a key tower. The officers in the other towers matched the key tower's lights as they changed by hand.

Soon another step in co-ordination was taken. Traffic lights on mast arms affixed to posts about five blocks apart were constructed between the towers. The mast arms were connected by underground electric wire to the key tower. Every time the key man operated a switch, all the lights along the avenue changed together. The first such remote control system in the world was put into operation July 10th, 1924, on Broadway between Rector Street and 86th Street.

Five years later, the final step in co-ordination was made when the key towers for each avenue were taken down and all systems were united under one control.

Manhattan's Traffic Control Station is in the 14th Police Precinct at 138 West 30th Street. It occupies a surprisingly small room. The fourteen traffic circuits of the Borough enter the fourteen control boxes in the following order:

1. York Ave.
2. 1st Ave.
3. 3rd Ave.
4. Lexington Ave.
5. Upper Park Ave.
6. 4th Ave.
7. Madison Ave.
8. Upper Fifth Ave.
9. Avenue of the Americas.
10. Seventh Ave. and Varick St.
11. 8th Avenue
12. 9th Avenue & Columbus Ave.
13. 10th and Amsterdam Aves.
14. Lower Fifth Ave.

The boxes control almost all the 4,000 traffic signals in Manhattan at 2,240 intersections. The connecting cables are laid in the conduits of the Empire City Electric and Telegraph Subway Company which permits the city to use one-tenth of its duct space.

Each cable has two spare wires for a temporary hook-up in case of failure of a line, until such time as a repair can be made by the maintenance men.

A mechanism composed of gears and cams revolved by a motor operates each circuit. As it closes the circuit, it causes a small switch in every one of the circuit's traffic posts to close the local circuit between a set of four bulbs and the Edison Light cable which passes through the post. The operating mechanism opens and closes a number of circuits causing the north and south lights to burn green for sixty seconds, followed by an interval of four seconds dark and all red. Meanwhile, the east and west lights burn red. Then, while the north and south lights are red, the east and west lights burn green for twenty-two seconds, followed by an interval of four seconds dark and all red. This repeats itself all through the twenty-four hours of the day. The traffic guides never sleep.

A sergeant and four operators comprise the staff of the control station. They are under the supervision of the Engineering Bureau of the Police Department. Not only do they attend to the proper operation of the control units, they are also headquarters for any trouble that develops anywhere in the Borough. Their maintenance men are out in the field. Every hour, these men telephone a report on their work and ask for further instructions.

When a police precinct calls up to report a signal out of order, the notice is posted in a log book and marked on the blackboard for action. The maintenance man is notified as soon as he calls. On completing his repair, he telephones to say so and the time is recorded in the log. This record is important in case of traffic accidents and is often requested by the courts. Every traffic signal has a card on which is kept a case history of its health, much like the case history a doctor makes of his patient.

The maintenance men also take care of the isolated traffic signals which are operated by electric clocks. It is important that these signals work in perfect time with the circuits. The maintenance men, therefore, whenever they telephone, check their stop watches with the station time. The station's motor-operated clock is checked with the Telephone Company at the beginning of every tour of duty.

Besides the synchronous or uniform circuit system, the City uses what is known as the progressive system. You've seen it. It is a circuit of traffic signals which alternates its green and red lights in such a way as to permit an automobile to keep moving at a uniform speed of about twenty miles an hour without crossing a red light. This system does not work well in congested areas, but is very satisfactory on wide roads whose traffic is not very heavy. It is in operation in Central Park, and, in the Borough of Brooklyn, on Ocean Parkway, Ocean Avenue, Clinton Street, Washington Avenue and Atlantic Avenue. The mechanism operating the progressive circuit is much the same as that operating the synchronous system.

If the traffic of the cities of the world moves with speed, smoothness and safety, the thank-you bow should be in the direction of the Police Department of the City of New York. However, it must be confessed that the Police Department was compelled to use its inventive powers or be overwhelmed by dangerous confusion. For nowhere in the world did the automobile multiply so rapidly. We simply had to be saved from its rocketing numbers. It is a curious fact that in modern times we often need an invention to rescue us from the consequences of another invention or to make it safe to use. In the case of the automobile, the remote-control traffic signal system has been the enabling answer. It is impossible to imagine the Automobile Age without it.


## Chapter 15

## Under Earth And Water

A CITY IS A PLACE of many goings. We go to work. We go to shop, we go to the theater, we go to visit and finally we go home. In New York City, over ten million people a day ride from place to place. Of these, seven million climb below streets into the subways and about three million people travel in street cars, buses, taxis and privately owned cars. And still the streets are terrifically congested!

Can you imagine the City going about its business without

the rapid transit of subways? Can you picture the tight confusion of ferry boats without the sixty-two bridges and sixteen tunnels that help carry the continuous traffic across the rivers? The water-ways would be like bottles packed full of sand—and the sand would not flow.

The toughest problem that any big city faces is to provide for reasonably fast circulation through its traffic arteries—and at a low cost. The history of public transportation within New York City begins in 1786 when the first horse-drawn cab was driven by its owner for hire. In 1800, the stagecoach appeared on the streets. Passengers paid twelve and one-half cents below 14th Street, eighteen and three-quarter cents to Yorkville, and twenty-five cents to Harlem and Manhattanville.

In 1832, the stagecoach was set on rails and became a horse-drawn omnibus. Steam-power trains came into the City as far down as 32nd Street. The City's population now began growing at a tremendous rate. The opening of the Erie Canal had made it the most important seaport in the land. Its northern boundary crept up from 14th Street to 23rd Street to 34th Street to 42nd Street. By the end of the Civil War, people were living away up at Central Park and having difficulty getting down to the business center below 14th Street. The streets were a tangle of all manner of vehicles. More space was needed on the streets, but every year saw less and less of it.

The first solution to this condition was the elevated railroad. In 1878, the Sixth Avenue El and the Third Avenue El thundered into being. Though steam drawn and belching smoke and cinders, the trains on stilts provided cheap and rapid transportation, and, best of all, took it off the surface of the too crowded streets.

More Els followed, but the City grew even more rapidly. Finally, it was decided to take part of the traffic underground. Electricity and electric motors had been developed far enough to make the idea of subway trains feasible. Indeed, beginning in 1900, street cars and El trains were gradually electrified.

As with any novel plan, some men sprang up to fight the proposal of subways. Russell Sage, one of the most powerful railroad financiers in the country, said it was "Ridiculous!" Owners of stock in the streetcar and El companies led the battle against going into "a hole in the ground." But they could not hold progress back. Ground was broken for the first subway early in 1900. Four years later the first train sped under the city streets from Brooklyn Bridge to 145th Street and Broadway.

Now the City seemed well on its way to solve the problem of many goings. Its streets had become three deckers: subway, road and El. In later years, when automobile traffic began to overwhelm it, its engineers built tunnels and elevated roadways to keep the rivers and streets from hopelessly jamming. To this day, however, in spite of Herculean efforts, the City has not caught up with the increasing millions who go so blithely about their business. Indeed, New Yorkers show off their crowded subways and are proud of the unequaled streams of vehicles that pour through their streets.

London is the mother of the slightly more than four hundred miles of subways that now tunnel under the streets of the great cities of the world. In 1862 and 1863 it constructed two experimental tunnels, hoping thus to find a way of taking some of the trucking traffic off its public highways. One was a pneumatic tube in which little cars ran on narrow rails and were blown back and forth by huge fans twenty-one feet in diameter. The other tunnel had a track width of seven feet along which the parcel-bearing cars were pulled by cables.

Inspired by London's example, Alfred E. Beach, editor of the Scientific American, obtained the right to construct a pneumatic parcels subway under the most congested section of Manhattan, from the southwest corner of Warren Street, down Broadway to a point nearly opposite the south side of Murray Street. During the tunneling it occurred to Beach that if parcels could be blown back and forth, so could passengers. When the tunnel was completed, the rails, the car and the blowing machinery installed, all the big men of the City came to make the first trip. That was in 1871.

Here's how the Scientific American described New York City's first subway:

"Let the reader imagine a cylindrical tube, eight feet in the clear, bricked up and whitewashed, neat, clean, dry and quiet. Along the bottom of this tube is laid a railroad track and on this track runs a spacious car, richly upholstered, well lighted and with plenty of space for exits. The track is single and level; it is not cold in winter. It will be delightfully cool in summer. The filthy health-destroying street dust will never be found in the tunnel."

In spite of Beach's enthusiasm, his idea made no further headway. Nor did London extend its experiments to passenger traffic. The simple fact is that a practical underground railway awaited the development of electricity.

In 1890, London again showed the way when the City and South London Railway opened the initial section of the first true passenger subway in the world. The cars were electrically powered. Because they were designed to run through the earth, they had no windows! Naturally!

Ten years later, New York City, profiting by London's experience in subway building, sank its first subway shaft at City Hall. Since then it has built 133 miles of subway tunnel to London's 79 miles and Paris' 70 miles.

The originally privately owned operating companies, the IRT and the BMT, were bought by the City in 1940 and merged with its Independent System into one municipally owned system oper-

ated by the Board of Transportation of the City of New York.
And now, let's build a subway.

The job of constructing a subway is one of the toughest and
most complicated in the engineering field. In New York City the
assignment of seeing it through, from discussion to paper plan to the
first official run, belongs to the Board of Transportation.

The first thing its engineers do is plot the route of the tunnel. While one gang of men takes borings of the earth through
which the tunnel will be cut or blasted, another group of field men
makes a complete map of all the obstacles and hazards which the
tunneling will encounter.

This survey indicates the relative location, depth and size of
every manhole and vault; of all gas and water mains, sewers and
electric transformers; of all cables, conduits and duct banks of
electricity, of the telephone, telegraph, police and fire telegraph

systems, and of the traffic signal system; of the pneumatic tubes, trolley third rails and possible tunnels that underlie the proposed route. Every sidewalk opening along the way will be recorded: cellars, vaults, coal holes and oil pipes. Every light pole, telegraph pole, bridge support and El column will be indicated. Every building on the route will be carefully described. The buildings form a special problem. They must be protected against shifting, cracking walls or the possibility of sliding into the excavation.

This survey and the information on soil conditions obtained from the borings enable the Designs Division of the Board of Transportation to determine the most suitable and economical location, size and form of the subway. The borings are also of first importance to the contractors who in bidding for the job must know whether they will be digging, blasting, or cutting their way through under compressed air, the most expensive of all methods. They must also have the obstacle survey to help them understand the size of their task.

Later, the survey will assume a new importance. It will prevent the kind of destructive accident that would follow a driller's blindly boring into an unseen gas main or an electric shovel's smashing into a hidden twenty-foot water main. Subway engineers pride themselves on the fact that life goes on about the street much as always in spite of the tremendous job they are doing.

When the squads of engineers who design each section of subway have completed their drawings, the prints are bound into a volume which accompanies the graciously titled "Invitations to Contractors." The contractors must all be responsible and experienced. The lowest bidder for each section is awarded the contract. The Board of Transportation now examines the bids and the Board of Estimate votes the necessary funds.

Even as the contractor puts up his field offices, his first-aid clinics, his carpenter and machine shops, his air compressors, hydraulic pumps and storage magazines for explosives, the steel mills begin to fabricate the girders, rails and other metal parts that will later be required. Throughout the construction, Board of Transportation engineers and inspectors supervise and watch its progress, test all materials and advise on all problems.

As we have already learned in aqueduct building, there are

three ways of cutting a tunnel. The preferred method is the cut-and-cover, which simply requires digging an open trench to the depth of the tunnel floor, constructing the tunnel in it, and restoring the street surface.

When, however, the tunnel dives under other tunnels or runs into hills or valleys that would require the train to climb a grade more than four feet in a hundred feet, the tunnel must be cut too deep for mere cut-and-cover. It is then tunneled or bored through from shaft to shaft, most often without disturbing the surface of the street or the services that underlie the surface.

The third method, that of the shield pushing forward under compressed air conditions, is made necessary when tunneling through faulty rock or mushy earth, or under rivers. The expanding force of the compressed air keeps the earth and water from bursting into the tunnel and sweeping over men and machines.

And now let's pick up our drills and shovels and follow a cut-and-cover operation. If there is any heavy blasting to be done, all large windows on the street are fitted at the center with a wooden cross held in place by wires that extend to the four corners of the window frame. In case of a blast, the wooden support, or spider, will keep the center of the pane from vibrating. The four parts of the pane that will vibrate will thus be unable to add their vibrations together and so shatter the pane.

Another thing that must be done before the asphalt can be cut into is to remove the gas mains from the danger zone. New gas pipes are laid against the sidewalk curb and covered over by wooden steps. Where huge gas mains cross the line of construction, equally large mains supported by wooden towers are by-passed fourteen feet above the street.

When the emergency mains have all been laid, they are very carefully connected to the old mains. The building connections are then transferred to the new mains and the two systems are disconnected. When all remaining gas in the old system has been sucked back into the gas holders, its mains are no longer a fire hazard. They are dead.

Now the actual operation begins. The subway surgeons cut through the skin of the street, exposing the service organs and intestines layer by layer. However, unlike the surgeon operating on you or me, their job is not to cut out a part but to put in an organ that has not been there.

Only one third of the width of the street is uncovered at a time, leaving the rest of the road to traffic, and even this third is bridged or decked as soon as possible. Heavy beams or steel piles are driven into the earth, ten or more feet apart. Other beams or girders are laid across the piles to form the framework for the deck of the temporary roadway.

As each wire, pipe and cable is uncovered, it is hung from this framework by rope or wire. The very large water mains are provided with concrete or steel legs that go down below the depth of the tunnel. As for the old brick and concrete sewers that cannot be so supported, they are broken in from the top and new iron pipe sewers are laid inside. The pipe is suspended from the cross-

beams and the sewage is then routed into it.  New veins for old!
No surgeon could do the same for us.

While this is going on, crews of engineers and workmen are
underpinning the buildings along the streets.  Your legs are your
pins.  Underpinning, then, is the act of providing legs.  The very
big buildings, such as skyscrapers, usually rest on steel piers that are
firmly anchored on bedrock.  It is the smaller buildings, many of
them merely set above their cellars with no other anchorage, that
must be underpinned to bedrock or at least to firm soil which will
not be disturbed by the construction of the subway.

Monuments, El supports and bridge piers along the line of
excavation are also provided with stilts that will permit them to
stand on unshakeable ground.

The excavation, having gone about seven feet deep along the
length of a block, is now decked with steel or heavy wooden beams.
The bridge above the cut must be strong enough to withstand not
only the usual traffic of the street but the added weight of the
contractor's power cranes, shovels and heavily loaded trucks.  The
decking is so laid that any part of it may be removed to provide
access to where the men are working.

Usually, handpicks and shovels are the first to attack the earth. Now power shovels scoop into it. Rock, of course, is blasted away. Many holes are drilled into it. Dynamite sticks are placed in these holes. Electric wires interconnect the explosive and lead to a blasting box a safe distance away. When all is in readiness, a heavy steel blanket is placed over the blasting area, a man at the blasting box throws the switch, an electric spark shoots out to every stick of dynamite; there is a tremendous roar—and under the thrashing blanket lies the rock now crumbled small enough to be carted away.

Sometimes the cut has to be worked as from a shaft. Whenever possible, however, a ramp is built down to it so that shovels and trucks can descend into it directly.

The City, lying almost at sea level, has a very leaky body. The floor of the subway is seldom less than twenty-five feet and sometimes seventy-five feet below the street surface. No wonder water is constantly seeping into the cut. Even the rock leaks! Drainage ditches are, therefore, dug to carry the water off to collecting sumps from which it is pumped into the street sewer. As the excavation progresses, the walls are shored up as in a mine.

Digging the subway in earth is a cold, wet, muddy job. Tunneling through rock is scarcely better because of the terrific racket of drills and the dangerous clouds of rock dust. The men have always to watch for rotten rock that may loosen and fall upon them. The only fresh air comes down the shafts and the air vents that are bored through to the street every block or so. Subway building is a job for which no sissy need apply.

As soon as the rock tunnel has gone some distance, a miniature railroad is built to speed up the clearing away of blasted rock. Small cars, powered by storage batteries and fitted with detachable buckets, haul the rock to the shaft. A powerful crane on the street reaches down, seizes a bucket at a time and drops the contents into a waiting truck. It is drill, blast, haul and often shore until the single track tunnel or four track tunnel with stations is driven through.

Possibly the most dangerous, punishing work in the world is shield tunneling under compressed air conditions. Only husky young men in perfect physical shape can work and remain healthy under air pressures of from ten to fifty pounds per square inch.

London invented and developed the shield. The New York and New Jersey Railroad Company was the first in the United States to use it when, in 1874, it tried to put through the Hudson-Manhattan Tunnel under the Hudson River. However, all sorts of difficulties developed due to inexperience and inability to apply equal air pressure to the top and bottom of the shield. After many minor floodings and silt slides, a major slide invaded the shield and blocked the exits. Twenty men were drowned. This was in 1880.

Not until 1902 did the company have courage enough to resume the work. By this time the contractors knew a great deal more about shield tunneling. The East River Gas Tunnel had been successfully holed through eight years earlier. A subway tunnel was being pushed across under the Harlem River to the Bronx. Another subway tunnel was being driven across the East River to Brooklyn. The Pennsylvania Railroad was about to begin work on its great tunnels crossing under the waters of the Hudson to New Jersey.

Indeed, shield tunneling was becoming as nearly a routine method as cut-and-cover. Nearly, but never quite. Let's go down an air tunnel shaft and see what the men are about.

Over the point where the air tunneling will begin, a huge caisson is constructed. This is actually a square shield, heading downward into the earth, its four walls ground to a sharp edge at the bottom to cut into the earth, its upper structure heavily weighted to force the cutting edges down. When the caisson reaches the floor level of the projected tunnel, the tunnel air shield is built into it. This shield is a powerful steel and iron ring whose inside diameter is slightly larger than the outside diameter of the projected tunnel. To bolster it further against the enormous pressures of silt and water around it, steel girders support it in the same way that the spokes of a wheel keep the wheel rim from collapsing.

The shield front has two decks from which the men can excavate. The upper deck can be pushed out to the tunnel heading. The upper half of the front forms a semi-circular hood over the men, protecting them from falling rock and silt. Around the rim of the front and of the tail of the shield are powerful hydraulic jacks which we shall soon see at work.  The tail of the shield also carries a short crane, the erector arm.

When the shield has been pushed forward enough to allow for further construction, a very thick concrete wall or bulkhead is built into the mouth of the tunnel, closing it completely.  Its purpose is to make airtight the tunnel between it and the shield. This wall is so thick that it has three chambers or locks built into it: the muck lock, the man lock and the emergency lock.  Larger shields may have more and larger locks.  The caisson is also equipped with airlocks.  As the tunneling proceeds, new bulkheads are built complete with airlocks every 350 or 500 feet in order to maintain air pressure.  The rear bulkhead is cleared away, being no longer needed.

Now we are ready to put on the air pressure and begin pushing the shield forward under the river bottom.  Before the sand hogs can enter the tunnel, however, they must go into the man lock.  When they are all in this boiler-like tube, the door is locked and the air pressure is slowly increased.  Thus the men become gradually used to the great weight of the atmosphere in which they will work.

The period in the man lock will be anywhere from seven minutes for fifteen pounds of air pressure to half an hour for forty-five pounds. Without this adjustment the men would become very sick and might even die. When the pressure on the men reaches the pressure in the tunnel, the door into the tunnel is opened and the men proceed to their work.

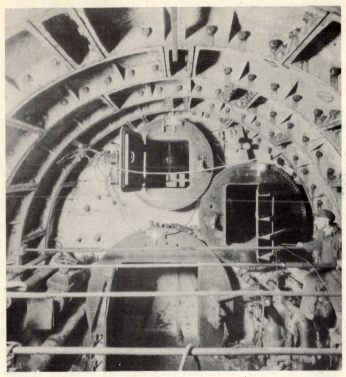

If the shield is heading into muck and sand, boards are placed against the heading to keep it from caving into the shield. The boards are held in place by the front hydraulic jacks. The men excavate by removing one board at a time. Should they remove more in loose soil, there is danger of the air pressure blowing right out into the river above this soil and blowing the miner with it. This has happened.

When the men have filled the cars of the muck train, the driver takes it in to the muck lock and gets back into the tunnel. The lock is regulated from the outside. The door is automatically shut and the outside door is opened. Out comes the compressed air with a tremendous roar. The cars are rolled out and are unloaded by the crane above the shaft.

On the return journey the cars re-enter the lock, the door is shut and the full tunnel air pressure is at once applied. The cars, of course, do not need to adjust themselves. But if the muck lock were opened while its atmosphere was normally low, the compressed atmosphere in the tunnel would rush into it. The result would be disaster! The invisible hands of air that keep out the river having suddenly been withdrawn, the silt and water would pour into the tunnel and overwhelm the men. Occasionally the tunnel is flooded.

The men race along a cat walk at the top of the tunnel back to the bulkhead and pop into the emergency lock. The lock is under the same air pressure as the tunnel. As soon as they have shut the door, the pressure is slowly reduced. When it is at normal the men go out into the shaft to safety. The emergency lock has saved many a man's life.

At best, working in air is hot, oppressive and tiring. Under the lower compressed air pressures, men can go on digging, loading, bolting and so on for three hours at a time. But when pressures of forty to fifty pounds are applied, the men can stand only half-hour periods of work. When time is called, they re-enter the man lock and are slowly decompressed from the pressure they have had to bear.

This process is of tremendous importance. If it is too jumpy, or hasty, bubbles of oxygen will form in the blood. This will give the victim the dreaded "bends," crippling him and perhaps killing him. The lock attendant has a grave responsibility indeed. The Labor Law requires that decompression should not be faster than one minute for each pound of pressure.

When the shield has been pushed forward about three feet, the erector arm on its tail puts into place the cast iron and steel segments of the shell of the permanent tunnel. These segments have been made true to the drawings, are all numbered and fit perfectly. The ring they form is about thirty-two inches wide. It is securely bolted together and bolted also to the ring beside it. When the excavation has proceeded another three feet, the powerful jacks on the inside rim of the shield are propped against the new ring, hydraulic pressure is applied and the jacks slowly push the shield out into the cleared heading. Again the erector arm sets up a ring sector of the tunnel shell.

In order to fix the shell firmly in the outer earth and rock, the men force a thin cement or sometimes gravel through holes in the shell. You remember this grouting process in the aqueduct tunnels. It fills all the holes directly outside and freezes the tunnel into its surroundings.

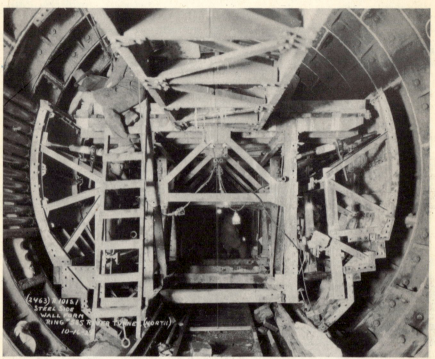

As in land tunnels, workmen start on both sides of the river at the same time and bore toward each other. The great moment is when they hole through! So accurate is the course they cut, that tunnels, even when they curve, seldom have more than an inch of difference between their opposite sections.

Getting back to the cut-and-cover trenches, when they are several blocks long, concrete mixing trucks pour their contents of sand, cement, water and crushed stone down funnels into the raw cuts. A floor of concrete one foot deep is laid. Higher ridges or benches are built up where the supporting columns will be set; that is, along the walls and, if the tunnel is wide, in the center.

As soon as the concrete has dried hard, the steel roof beams of the subway are riveted to the columns about five feet apart. Wooden forms are built between the wall girders and between the crossbeams that form the roof and the tunnel receives an all around skin of concrete. The middle columns are left naked unless they are to become part of a collision wall, a wall that will prevent a de-railed train from climbing to the neighboring track. In the rock tunnels, as in the shield tunnels, the outside spaces are thoroughly grouted.

The concrete station platforms are now poured and the duct banks of tile tubing installed. These tubes will carry all the cables and wiring that the subway needs for its lighting, its signal system and its telephone network.

When necessary, and in New York City that is almost always, the outside walls of the concrete shell are heavily water-proofed with layers of asphalted cotton cloth.

The excavator's main job is now complete. He has only to restore the street above the cut-and-cover tunnel. Only! But what a job! First he fills in and tamps down the earth all about the tunnel. This must be thorough enough to prevent later settling. Then in close co-operation with the engineering departments of the water, sewer, gas, steam, electric and communications services, he replaces pipes, ducts, manholes, vaults, and everything else that he shifted or destroyed.  He also rebuilds the building vaults which he had to invade.

Last of all, he removes the battered decking, fills earth solidly around all structures, and lays a new street and new sidewalks.

He is through at last! He has done a good job.  The rest is up to a whole host of other contractors.  But already the first train trip may be said to be in sight.

The men who plot the tracks must plot not well—but perfectly. And they do.  Their highly exacting work begins just as soon as the course and grades of the subway have been decided.  They must design the rails for all comings and goings, crossings and switchings. They must tell the manufacturer of rails whether to make them straight or bend them and exactly how much up or down, left or right.

Long before the excavator has cleaned up his job, the track sections, together with the sections of third rail, begin arriving.  The rails are laid on short ties of waterproofed pine and fastened to them by screws and tie plates.  Then the space between each pair of ties and beyond them to the wall of the tunnel is filled with concrete. Thus the tracks are fixed unshakeably into the tunnel.

If you will look at the tracks next time you are on a subway station, you will notice that there is no concrete filling between the opposing rows of ties. This channel drains whatever water gets into the tunnel into the collecting sumps from which it is pumped into the sewers. And, occasionally, this channel has saved the lives of people who have fallen off the station platform.

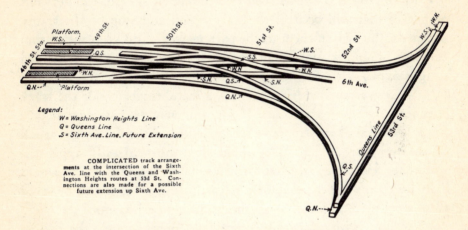

Legend:
W = Washington Heights Line
Q = Queens Line
S = Sixth Ave. Line. Future Extension

COMPLICATED track arrangements at the intersection of the Sixth Ave. line with the Queens and Washington Heights routes at 53d St. Connections are also made for a possible future extension up Sixth Ave.

While I was writing this chapter, one of Uncle Sam's sailors dropped into the trough and fell fast asleep! It was long past midnight, the station was deserted and he was not at once noticed. Two trains thundered over him and still he slumbered on. When the motorman of the third train saw the body between the tracks, he pulled the brakes. But too late. The train jolted to a stop several cars past the body. The horrified motorman and the guards hurried to extricate the mangled remains. Instead, they had great difficulty in waking the heroic sleeper. Except for a few scratches and a justifiable loss of temper at being awakened, he was as whole as ever!

The track is finished with the laying of the third rail. This electric conductor is spiked through every fifth tie. A metal connection or bond bridges the thin space between each section of rail in order to insure an uninterrupted flow of current. Since an electric current can only exist in a circuit, the negative return of electricity is made through one of the rails of the actual track. This track must also be bonded.

Interestingly enough, the other rail also acts as a negative conductor. It completes the circuit for the signal system. In other words, all three tracks are electrically charged, but only the one with the wooden guard is dangerous. That rail is a killer.

While the track is being put down, other contractors are busy tiling walls, cementing platforms, constructing toilets, building entrances and stairs, and installing the ventilating system, the lighting system, the change booths and the turnstiles.

Most vital is the installation of the signal system, the network of nerves that will control the start, speed and stop of the trains, automatically switch them to the correct track and keep them from colliding should a motorman for some reason fail to see the red danger signal.

Whenever the red light goes on, a metal finger beside the track rises several inches above it. If a train were to pass over it, the finger would strike a trip valve suspended from the first wheel truck of the first car. The valve would then automatically apply the air brakes and arrest the motorman's power switch. This would halt the train with the snap of a released spring. It would be saved from a collision, because, of all things, it had been tripped up!

At last, with everything complete, down comes the rolling stock. The Board of Transportation engineers make the final tests, checking and re-checking every detail.

And finally, four or five years after the first sample bore was made, comes the great day! New Yorkers tumble through the shiny turnstiles, examining, admiring and approving. The subway roars with the song it will be singing for scores of years. If it is a hot summer day every one will praise the engineers who built the tunnel for its delightful coolness, not knowing that it takes a subway about seven years to equal the surface temperatures. The Board of Transportation will look on and be justly happy at a job well done—and turn away to begin a new one. New York City has never had enough subways.

The subways, of course, do not help with the growing congestion of private cars, motor trucks and buses that daily use its streets. Two commissions do their best to cope with this problem. One is the New York City Tunnel Authority which has the task of providing speedier avenues of transportation within the five boroughs of the city. The other and older body is the Port of New York Authority.

and, so far as reasonable, the passage of through traffic by tunnels and overpasses so that the streets and the rivers may be as free as possible.

Underneath Grand Central Station

The map on the following page is a simplification of one of the most complex underground areas in the world.

Grand Central Station was begun in 1903 on the site of the old depot and opened in 1913. Full electrification was completed in 1907. But as far back as 1871, in the days of steam and open tracks, the old depot was never defiled by soot and cinders. Locomotives picked up speed before reaching the last switch, were uncoupled and switched off, and the cars behind them rolled into the depot on their own momentum!

Three signal towers control the five miles of four tracks from the Mott Haven Yard down Park Avenue to 57th Street. At this point, twenty feet below the sidewalk, the through trains enter a fan of forty-one tracks to the station. Suburban trains dive twenty-four feet below this maze to a fan of twenty-six tracks.

Grand Central is the only terminal in the world with two levels of tracks and loops on which trains may go out without being backed out. Thirty-four miles of track traverse the three-quarter-mile stretch of the station yard servicing about two hundred thousand passengers in five hundred daily trains.

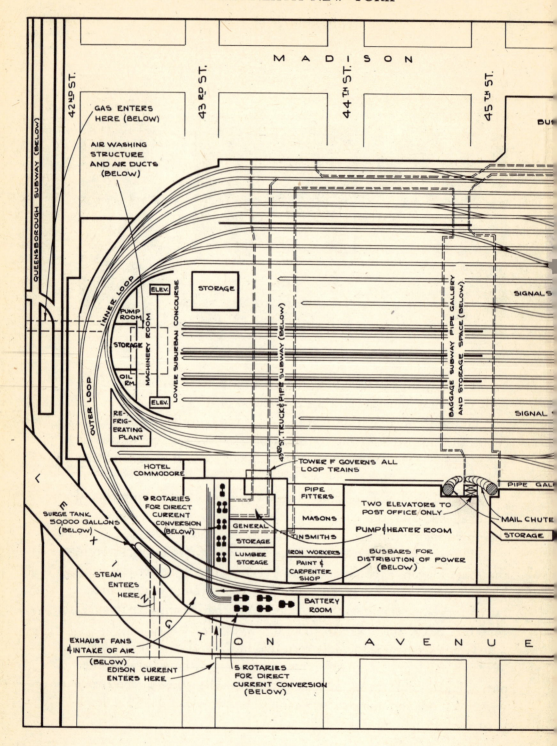

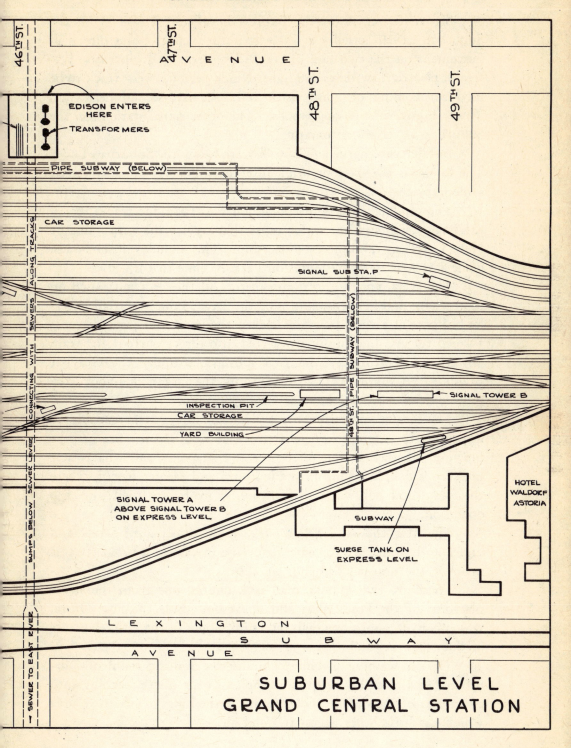

SUBURBAN LEVEL
GRAND CENTRAL STATION

Signal Tower A on the Express Level and Tower B on the Suburban Level, actually a single structure, control and direct all movement on the two fans of tracks by means of an intricate system of electrical switches and lights which permits every track to be used for coming or going with trains at five-second headways. Tower F governs the loop tracks. The other signal stations on the Suburban Level are automatic.

Installations marked (BELOW) are below the Suburban Level. The lowest is the six-foot brick intercepting sewer at 46th Street, some sixty feet below streets.

The pipe galleries, some of which underpass the tracks, carry the huge steam and hot water pipes that service the entire area of New York Central Railroad ownership. This includes all the hotels, office and apartment buildings on Park Avenue to 59th Street.

The New York Central also meters all the electricity used on its trackage and in the buildings of the area. Edison current enters its bus bars at several points at eleven thousand volts and is transformed for AC lighting or converted into direct current for train power and lighting by the two substations under the Graybar Building. A number of battery rooms, the largest one above the nine rotaries, store one hour of emergency power.

The largest substation has a fire signaling system capable of informing the engineers on what track at what street a fire may be burning, whether to shut off power at that point, and what water pressure is desired. Pumps in the Pump and Heater Room, where the steam and hot water distribution is made, are then put into operation.

The fifty thousand gallon surge tanks under 43rd Street and under 49th Street are for emergency use in case of a broken water main or the unusual demands of a fire.

There are two gravity mail-sack chutes, one from the street platform of the Post Office and one from inside the Post Office, which converge into one delivery chute opposite the P.O. elevators on Suburban Level.

The air washing machinery under the waiting room of Suburban Level, together with its complex of air ducts reaching into every part of the station underground, is the lungs of life to an area which has little other access to good air.

# PART VII

# CONCLUSION

# Chapter 16

## City Of The Future

*I dream'd in a dream, I saw a city invincible
    to the attacks of the whole of the rest
    of the earth;
I dream'd that was the new City of Friends.*

—Walt Whitman

WELL, HERE WE ARE AT THE END of our description of the physiology of a modern city and how it got that way. But now that we know more about what lies under the city's skin than a water-supply engineer or a power engineer or a telephone engineer would know without this book, it is time to remind ourselves that above sanitation and power and communications and transportation, a city is *people*. This chapter is about people living in a city; it is about you and your family. It could be any city, just as the book applies generally to any city in the world; specifically, however, it is about New York City.

The fact is that though science, invention and engineering have done an amazing job of servicing their minimum needs, cities are still far from being the best places to live in. It isn't a matter of more sewers or subways or fire protection, however important these may be. It is simply that the modern city grew up higgeldy-piggeldy.

Many ancient cities were planned. Athens was planned; it was easier, then. Peter the Great planned St. Petersburg, now Leningrad. Washington, D.C., was a planned city. William Penn laid out Philadelphia and Gouvernier Morris made some effort to control New York City's development. But all this was long before the industrial era. On the whole, the cities of the world just grew from village to metropolis with no overall plan, no vision of future needs. Indeed, the village cows often determined the street pattern of the city-to-be.

203

New York is an example of a city that has been improving itself all through the three hundred years of its existence, but piece-meal, now in one department, now in another, without any control of the whole design.

Its business, financial and wholesale houses, its largest department stores and retail establishments, its hotels and amusements, are for the most part concentrated in the bottom of the Manhattan sock. There are buildings in this skyscraper area that have a day-time population of thirty thousand people. Every work morning, over a million persons funnel into this area by subway, bus, car, commuter train and ferry—and in the evening, have to fight their way home again some hour's distance or more away. The streets and avenues, wide enough in the horse and buggy era, are too narrow for present-day traffic.

Forty percent of the city's dwellings are over forty years old; some slum areas are 50 to 70 years old. Their flats are small, without sufficient light and closet space; many have no bathroom; some share a hall toilet; they are in disrepair, infested with vermin and they breed disease and crime. In many places, these foul slums and the apartment houses of the wealthy are fantastically mixed. Jim Crow has jammed six hundred people on some of Harlem's acres where two hundred could not live comfortably.

The City has not enough school space nor playgrounds. It suffers from many other faults due to its planless growth and the unchallenged right, until recently, of anyone to build whatever he pleased anywhere that suited him without regard to the community's best interest.

You could make the same criticism of nearly all the cities in the world.

Only after the first World War, when New York City had its most active building boom, did the municipal government move to defend the common rights and comforts of all the people. It created the zoning law and rewrote the housing laws. In consequence, new skyscrapers had to have setbacks in order not to rob their neighbors of too much light and air; all areas of the city were restricted in their new residential and business structures, their height and the percentage of the total land space they could occupy;

every room in a new apartment house had to have a window admitting sufficient light and air.

Of course, this was not yet city planning. In fact, the new building developments spread in every direction and the weight of lower Manhattan's skyscraper population practically doubled, creating new problems of transportation and traffic flow.

At last, after much pressure by sociologists, economists, architects, artists, industrial engineers and just plain people, the City set up the New York City Planning Commission under the new charter adopted in 1936. The Commission actually began work in 1938. It consists of the Chief Engineer of the Board of Estimate and five members, one of whom is appointed Chairman by the Mayor. Its purpose is "to guide and to influence the City in its development and further growth." For this it studies the needs of the City as a whole, receives recommendations and plans from all departments of the City government, conducts public hearings on every related matter and puts its judgments down in the form of Master Plans which will some day cover all the problems of this largest of world cities. In the words of Cleveland Rodgers, one of the Commissioners and author of "New York Plans For The Future," it is the most complex kind of a job requiring "imagination, long reflection and much questioning" before even a tentative judgment can be made.

Increasingly, city dwellers all over the world are beginning to think of the inherited problems of their communities and to demand some planning so that these communities may become more efficient as machines for living. Even before the war against fascism, the Soviet Union built many new cities from the grass roots up. And of course, during the Nazi invasion of the Soviet Union's most industrialized area, entire cities were stripped of their industrial plants and together with the workers and their families transported beyond the Ural Mountains to new cities, specifically planned to receive them.

During the war, we, too, built new cities around war industries. Oak Ridge, Tennessee, the atom-bomb town, is a good example of a planned city. But our best experience in planning urban communities was before the war in the area of the Tennessee Valley Authority where government-owned cheap water power transformed the lives of a poverty-stricken, hopeless people into a richly useful, productive, hopeful pattern.

Hike down there some vacation time. See it for yourself; there is not its like anywhere in this country. Talk to the older people. Their stories will sound like incredible rags to riches tales—not money riches, but the riches of full, dignified living. Government planning did that for them. It succeeded against the most desperate kind of resistance by selfish interests not only in the five states of the TVA but from all over the country. It could not have succeeded without the long fight made for it by the common people of the TVA and of the rest of the country. David Lilienthal, the fighting head of the TVA and one of the world's most brilliant planners, acknowledged the people's share in the victory and even warned them not to become complacent. "The test of democratic planning," he told them, "is whether the people will fight for it—not simply whether they will accept it, or approve it or join in it—*but whether they will fight for it.*"

In Europe, many war-smashed cities are already beginning to rise from their rubble and ashes. Unquestionably, many of them will be rebuilt according to an overall plan that will seek to avoid recreating the problems from which their inhabitants once suffered.

Bomb-shattered London has a Greater London Plan which was adopted even before the war was over. Londoners think the city has too many people in it for good living. Therefore, no new industry will be allowed to enter London. Moreover, the municipality will remove 1,720 factories and their 258,000 employees and their families into eight satellite towns which it intends to build around itself like the moons around Saturn. These towns will house sixty thousand people each and each will be self-sufficient in every requirement of urban life: schools, shopping, theaters, churches, stadium, libraries and ways of earning a living.

As to the rebuilding of some of its damaged areas, the London plan is to organize them into neighborhood units housing 6,000 to 10,000 people, enough to maintain an elementary school and a shopping center. London through-motor-traffic will by-pass these units. The local streets will form a spider web design connecting with roads leading to the heart of the big city. There will be between 100 and 200 people per acre and the recreational areas and parks will come to no less than three acres for every thousand people. Together with the rest of the open space planned in London, play space will actually be ten acres per thousand people as compared to New York City's present day three acres per thousand.

Moscow also considers itself in danger of growing too large in population. It plans to limit itself to five million people, to exclude new industries, and to surround itself with a heavy belt of forest as further evidence of determination to limit its growth. It, too, plans to rebuild its residential areas into small neighborhood units complete with every urban need. It plans to save a great deal of space for recreational purposes by having its street blocks four and eight times as large as ours. As in London, local streets will be spider webbed and will connect to streets leading to the center of the city. All this will make local traffic conditions much lighter and therefore safer. Furthermore, both London and Moscow neighborhood units will have many dead-end streets, entirely removing them from traffic flow and traffic dangers. Living in Moscow and London is bound to be more comfortable, healthier, less time-wasting and more neighborly than before the war.

What are New York City's plans? Fortunately for us, we have no bombed-out areas. On the other hand, barring another war, much of New York City is here to stay a long time. The concern of the Planning Commission is how to guide changes and growth of the City without interrupting its life and to make plans that will be acceptable to the conflicting interests and desires of many groups. Its most pressing and difficult problem is how to get people to and from their work, their shopping and amusements in the least possible time over the shortest possible distance. It is a body of practical men looking no further ahead than twenty years because it knows that it cannot plan in 1950 for the unknown conditions of the year 2000 with its new energies and undreamed of tools and materials.

Its post-war plans involve the huge expenditure of more than a billion and a quarter dollars covering, among other matters, new schools and libraries, new health and hospital facilities, new public markets, parks, bridges, highways, traffic tunnels, sewage disposal plants, improved transportation, additional water supply—and new housing.

Possibly the most vital of these projects is new housing, and it is under the direction of the New York City Housing Authority. There are planned 16 housing units providing many thousands of apartments at cheap rentals with plenty of light and air, having the most modern conveniences, and sharing such advantages as community nurseries, solariums and auditoriums. They will have their own internal design of walks and lawns and play space—and no through-traffic streets. Together with the huge project being built by the Metropolitan Life Insurance Company and known as Stuyvesant Town, these new housing units will replace some of the worst slums of the City. Four of these units and Stuyvesant Town will be east of the government buildings, the financial and business skyscraper pocket and the wholesale district of Manhattan below 23rd Street. Two of the units will be on the west flank of the district north of this, comprising a dense concentration of wholesale houses, factories, department stores and retail shops, office skyscrapers and the restaurant and amusement center of the City. Two more units will be in Brooklyn, a short subway ride from lower Manhattan. These eight housing projects should do much to bring the workers in lower Manhattan closer to their daily work and so relieve some of the present transportation and traffic tangles.

But with all this master planning by the Planning Commission, it is still not overall planning: it is piecemeal planning and it is not good enough for you and me. The trouble is that government planning is still new in our country and it has to move gingerly among many prejudices and much selfish opposition to it. There is even a member of the present Planning Commission, one of its shrewdest and ablest men, who does not believe in city planning!

Well, we have seen what cities were like one hundred and fifty years ago when men did not yet know the value of clean water and proper sanitation and before the era of steam and gas and electricity and power tools and concrete and steel. What will cities be like one hundred and fifty years hence?

Some scenic designers and industrial engineers and visionary architects have made beautiful drawings of wonderfully clean, airy cities with skyscraper communities reaching a mile into the sky, ten blocks between every skyscraper, planes and helicopters gracefully landing on them, lifting from them; and far below, double- and triple-decker highways, some of them plunging through the second and third stories of the buildings.

These dreamers may be right; I wouldn't know. Of this we can be certain: we are at the beginning of the age of atomic energy and of new engines and of utterly new materials such as plastics, fantastically light powerful steels, even of elements whose atomic structures have been juggled. Indeed, the city of year 2100 may well be further removed from the city of today than was the city of 1800.

And this we also know—and we must take it deeply to heart: there will be no cities, there will not be many people left on this ancient planet if you and I and our parents and friends allow another war to be fought. For the first time in history a war brought death and destruction to cities and people hundreds and even thousands of miles distant from actual battlefronts. That was World War II. World War III will be inconceivably more devastating. No communities, no peoples will be safe from its rocket-propelled, radar-guided atomic bombs. There will be no victors in the next war, only a vast silence and death.

From now on, the peoples of the earth have to choose between the two most extreme choices the human race has ever had to make: total annihilation or, employing the same science, ascent to the most unimaginable heights of civilization and abundance.

There must not be another war.

You and I have a direct responsibility to see to it that war is never again made. We can do it. We must do it. Everyone of us, down to the six-year-olds collecting tin foil, took an active part in World War II. We must take an even more active part in the peace. We must see to it that our government remains friends with the rest of the governments of the earth—or we shall have no earth.

You and I have another responsibility if we and our children are to come into that future of beautiful life which is promised by atomic science. We must live in friendship among ourselves. That means we must regard our neighbors of whatever color or creed as having equal rights with us by reason of science and human justice and the Constitution of the United States in all the duties and privileges of American citizenship. It means we cannot afford the Harlem ghettos throughout the country. It means we must not allow our government to assist builders of new housing who dare exclude Negro families as was done in Stuyvesant Town.

We are a nation of many minorities of national origin, of race and of religion. Each of us must defend the others' right to the vote, to equally good housing and health, to equal job and educational opportunities—or we will end by not having any of these ourselves. We know where contempt of other peoples led the Germans under Hitler. It came mighty close to destroying us all.

Walt Whitman saw the truth of this during the Civil War. He knew then that only that city will be invincible to the attacks of the rest of the earth that will be the City of Friends, the city at peace within itself and with the rest of the world. In this day of the atomic bomb, this friendship becomes the first and most crucial requirement for personal and national existence.

For the sake of the shining cities of the Future, for our own sake and the sake of our children's children, you and I and all of us must never stop fighting for increasing friendship among ourselves and with the peoples of all the world.

This is the first book to describe the anatomy of a modern city, to tell how it developed, by what scientific and social principles, how it operates.

It could not have been written by any layman or any one engineer without the generous cooperation of many specialists in the informational and engineering personnel of the public utilities and the municipal departments of New York City. Not only did they supply the most vital historical, statistical and technical data and explanations, but each was good enough to check the material of his particular field to insure its accuracy.

Thanks to them, none of us need be like the cat who liked butter but could not recognize a churn.

Therefore, our most grateful acknowledgments

to Mr. L. P. Wood, Senior Civil Engineer, Board of Water Supply;

to Mr. R. H. Gould, Director, Division of Engineering and Architecture and to Mr. Fred Zeigler, Chief of the Hydraulic Section of the Department of Public Works and to Mrs. Minnie Graberson, Director of Sanitary Education of the Department of Sanitation for the chapter on sewage disposal;

to the information office and the many electrical, gas and steam engineers of the Consolidated Edison Company;

to Mr. Joseph F. Devaney and Engineer Frederick J. Linden of the New York Mail and Newspaper Transportation Company for the chapter on mail chutes;

to Mr. George P. Oslin, publicity director, Mr. J. R. Hyland, General Supervisor of the International Communications Department, and Mr. G. Hotchkiss, Co-ordinating Engineer, all of the Western Union Telegraph Company for the chapter on the telegraph;

to the information office and the engineers of the New York Telephone Company and the engineers of the A T & T Company and the Bell System for the chapter on the telephone;

to Mr. Val Fendrich, Chief of the Bureau of Fire Alarm Telegraph of the New York City Fire Department and to Mr. R. K. Hyde of the American District Telegraph Company for the chapter on fire protection;

to Inspector Francis Burns of the Telegraph Bureau of the New York City Police Department and to Engineer, Mr. Jacob Katz of the Traffic Bureau of the Police Department and to Mr. R. L. Loiseaux of the Holmes Electric Protective Company for the chapters on telegraphic police protection and the traffic signal system;

to Mr. Albert Goetz, Senior Civil Engineer of the Board of Transportation, to the engineers of the Tunnel Authority, for the chapter on subways and tunnels; to Mr. Harry Losee for his fine photographs;

to Assistant Engineer of the New York Central, Mr. F. W. Bingman for the most exciting guided tour of the book, the trip under Grand Central;

to Commissioner Cleveland Rodgers of the New York City Planning Commission;

to those who helped me research the background material for the book, most especially Mr. Emanuel Glassman, for his thorough work and enthusiasm;

and to Miss Barbara Chapman, whose editorial enthusiasm, encouragement and technical imagination helped make this book.